The
FABRIC
of HOPE

The FABRIC of HOPE

HOW GOD WEAVES REDEMPTION INTO EVERY SEASON

KIRBY KELLY

W Publishing Group

An Imprint of Thomas Nelson

The Fabric of Hope

© 2026 Kirby Kelly

All rights reserved. No portion of this book may be reproduced, stored in a retrieval system, or transmitted in any form or by any means—electronic, mechanical, photocopy, recording, scanning, or other—except for brief quotations in critical reviews or articles, without the prior written permission of the publisher.

Published in Nashville, Tennessee, by W Publishing, an imprint of Thomas Nelson.
W Publishing and Thomas Nelson are registered trademarks of HarperCollins Christian Publishing, Inc.

Published in association with The Bindery Agency, www.TheBinderyAgency.com.

Thomas Nelson titles may be purchased in bulk for educational, business, fund-raising, or sales promotional use. For information, please email SpecialMarkets@ThomasNelson.com.

Any internet addresses, phone numbers, or company or product information printed in this book are offered as a resource and are not intended in any way to be or to imply an endorsement by Thomas Nelson, nor does Thomas Nelson vouch for the existence, content, or services of these sites, phone numbers, companies, or products beyond the life of this book.

Unless otherwise noted, Scripture quotations are taken from the Holy Bible, New International Version®, NIV®. Copyright © 1973, 1978, 1984, 2011 by Biblica, Inc.® Used by permission of Zondervan. All rights reserved worldwide. www.zondervan.com. The "NIV" and "New International Version" are trademarks registered in the United States Patent and Trademark Office by Biblica, Inc.®

Scripture quotations marked CSB® are taken from the Christian Standard Bible®. Copyright © 2017 by Holman Bible Publishers. Used by permission. Christian Standard Bible® and CSB® are federally registered trademarks of Holman Bible Publishers.

Scripture quotations marked ESV are taken from the ESV® Bible (The Holy Bible, English Standard Version®). Copyright © 2001 by Crossway, a publishing ministry of Good News Publishers. All rights reserved.

Scripture quotations marked NKJV are taken from the New King James Version®. Copyright © 1982 by Thomas Nelson. Used by permission. All rights reserved.

Scripture quotations marked NLT are taken from the New Living Translation, Copyright © 1996, 2004, 2015 by Tyndale House Foundation. Used by permission of Tyndale House Publishers, Carol Stream, Illinois 60188. All rights reserved.

Without limiting the exclusive rights of any author, contributor, or the publisher of this publication, any unauthorized use of this publication to train generative artificial intelligence (AI) technologies is expressly prohibited. HarperCollins also exercise their rights under Article 4(3) of the Digital Single Market Directive 2019/790 and expressly reserve this publication from the text and data mining exception.

ISBN 978-1-4003-3777-4 (SC)
ISBN 978-1-4003-3779-8 (audiobook)
ISBN 978-1-4003-3778-1 (eBook)

Library of Congress Control Number: 2025951534

Printed in the United States of America
26 27 28 29 30 LBC 5 4 3 2 1

*To Richard, my beloved husband, who
is proof of the goodness of God,
the redemption of God, and the hope of God in my life.
I love you forever and always, my best friend!*

CONTENTS

1. When Life Chucks Lemons at Your Face 1
2. Blankies, Banners, and Burdens 13
3. God Is Fair, Life Is Not 27
4. Your Wounds Have a Why 43
5. When God Changes You, Not Your Circumstances 59
6. Faith Within the Fabric 77
7. When God's Will Doesn't Go Your Way 95
8. Let Hope Anchor Your Heart 113
9. Peace in the Pieces 131
10. Joy in the Journey 145
11. Every Wrong Made Right 163
12. What If God Doesn't Do It? 181
13. Restitched, Repurposed, and Rewritten 197

Acknowledgments 213
Notes 217
About the Author 223

Chapter 1

WHEN LIFE CHUCKS LEMONS AT YOUR FACE

I have always been one to find the good in everything. A glass-half-full kind of gal. Not delusional or in denial about all the brokenness of our world but genuinely hopeful, expectant, and excited for what is to come. I am convinced that every long climb I'll ever endure will end with a view that will take my breath away. You already know I'll drop the location on my Instagram so others get a preview of what awaits them if they choose to brave the trek themselves!

I have had many skeptics look at my glass-half-full of joy, peace, faith, and hope, and laugh in my face or troll my comment section. Why? Because my joy makes no sense. I get it. Something bad happens, and my response is to rejoice? Something I love is asked to be laid down or is taken from me, and I am willing to let it go? Something unexpected occurs that breaks my heart and shakes me to my core, yet I keep on believing? Something that is totally evil knocks me down and leaves me with scars, yet I still declare that my God is good? They think I am a fool! I really do get it. I may look like a fool for putting my faith in what is unseen, but my hope, peace, and joy in Christ have literally sustained me when the lemonade in my glass was a bit more sour than expected.

The reality is that life has chucked more than a handful of lemons at me. From being a child of divorced parents who both struggled with and died from addiction, to being severely bullied and abandoned by friends, to having my physical boundaries crossed by men—I have accumulated quite the stockpile of lemons. The doomsday preppers would be impressed at the sight of it, and the pirates of old would envy how little a threat scurvy is for me.

I know the lemons life has chucked at you haven't been easy either. Lemons of heartbreak, lemons of divorce, lemons of unfulfilled promises, lemons of unaccomplished dreams, lemons of devastating interruptions, or maybe even lemons of life-altering diagnoses.

Here's the thing about lemons that I think a lot of us have come to know and deeply hate: Even if you've got the tiniest, nearly undetectable cut on your hand, you'll feel the burn when the lemon juice comes into contact with it. We all want to get to the sweet, refreshing sip of lemonade that cools us down on a hot summer day, but sometimes pain reveals itself along the way. We feel tempted to quit altogether instead of pressing on, to ignore pain instead of acknowledging its presence, and to reach for the Country Time Lemonade instant powder instead of staying with the squeeze that leads to real refinement. The pressing is hard, the squeezing is uncomfortable, and the stings aren't delightful; but God's redemptive plan and unwavering presence through it all make the process worth it.

Even with my hands stinging from cuts and lemon juice, I refuse to quit trusting God to turn those dang lemons into something meaningful. I choose to make lemonade with Him. As I said, I know mixing some Country Time powder with a gallon of water would be way easier, but the truth is that the synthetic stuff is nothing like the real thing. Country Time isn't county fair lemonade; take it from a Texas girl. The real fresh-squeezed lemons that sting your hands as you slice them, the heaps of sugar that should send anyone into a coma, and the endless mixing are what make lemonade so much sweeter when the Texas sun seems to be melting your face off. I love me a cold glass of lemonade, but

> My glass has lemonade in it, and it's half full, but that's only because of a perspective shift.

I don't like the process of squeezing life's lemons to get there. Are you picking up what I'm putting down?

I understand that life has not dealt any of us an easy hand. We all have our scars and stories, our lemons, and our laments. All valid. All painful. But something meaningful, refreshing, and sweet can come out of the things life hands us. My glass has lemonade in it, and it's half full, but that's only because of a perspective shift. I now view life through the lens of God's redemptive plan woven throughout time: the biblical narrative and our individual stories. God is the silver lining that stitches the torn things back together, binding up our wounds and healing what has been hurt.

We all know that life will inevitably hand us some lemons. Sometimes life doesn't even have the common courtesy to hand them over but rather chucks them at our faces like a booing crowd in the Renaissance era. Life may chuck lemons at us, but God is the sugar that makes it worth something. He gives worth to what we see as nothing but waste. He gives sweetness to what was once a bitter taste. He is the joy, the peace, and the hope for our hurts. He is the Redeemer who brings purpose to the pain, glory to the shame, and relief from the strain of all your burdens. He has made all things beautiful, all things worth it, and all things new in my life, and I believe the same can be true for you.

He Restores What Feels Beyond Repair

I want to invite you to raise a glass with me, friend, because we can acknowledge the pain we've faced, both past and present, and still toast to a God who makes our lemons into lemonade. Maybe you're thinking that that sounds nice in theory, but sipping on lemonade and spotting the silver lining just isn't the most important thing on your to-do list today. Maybe life has not only tasted sour to you, but it has also been tainted with bitter tastes of betrayal, grief, unanswered prayers, and pain that feel absolutely irreconcilable with a sweet God. I don't want to rush past all the real stuff and make you put on a smiley-face mask. You can toast with tears. You can raise a glass while raising your questions and laments to the Lord. God isn't looking for you to "fake it till you make it" out of your woes. He is inviting you to honestly approach Him with everything, knowing that even with the bad, He can do something good. This is the hope we toast to. Even if you don't see it or believe it right now, that doesn't mean God is going to stop being who He is as the Redeemer of your story, right here, right now.

So, without further ado, allow me to kick off the chorus of toasts to the God we love by going first in this strange duality of hurt and hope. A chorus of coexisting in two places at once. Even while I was face down in the bottom of the pit of grief in this previous season of life, weeping and watering the ground with floods of tears, He met me there. He met me when the phone rang and I got the devastating news. He met me when I was told I had to be the decision-maker, "playing God" when everything felt out of my control. He met me when I was sitting alone outside with my Bible searching its pages for any type of answer, relief, or guidance. He met me when I had to hold my mother's hand as she took her final breath. He met me there as He met her, face-to-face, in glory. Cheers to the God who doesn't gaslight our grief, pass over our pain, or abandon us in our agony, but rather shows up in the unexpected, provides peace when it makes no sense, and causes beautiful things to bloom where it feels like no life was ever possible.

We are going to go there—to the parts of your own story that you've boxed up, tucked away in the basement, and haven't yet revisited because of what hurts might jump back out at you. The painful past, the disappointing present, and maybe the fearful future you're already bracing for. But there is good news. Though I haven't been where you've been or lived the life you've lived, I have seen one universal truth come to fruition in my story that I know will translate to yours: God can repurpose and restitch what once felt frayed, tattered, and too torn up to be redeemed. You are in for the greatest journey and most glorious surprise—the hand of God skillfully and intentionally at work, mending the messes to be masterfully meaningful. So let's go there—to the box in the basement you've tucked away, ignored, or tried to block out of your story. Let's reexamine it once more, but this time, in the light, and in the hands of a gentle Savior who takes the things we thought were beyond repair and restores them into something greater. He did it with me. I know He can do it again with you.

Nothing Is Wasted in God's Hands

I get that the easier thing to do is to stiff-arm the suffering, dread the difficulties, and ignore the instances we wouldn't wish on our worst enemy. The harder thing, but the more fruitful and beneficial thing you can do for yourself and your future, is to look at the season you're in and ask God, "Lord, what do You want to do in me, through me, and for me while I am here?" Nothing is wasted with God. When I look back at my seasons of difficulty, you bet I shed some tears, cringe at myself, and ache at the mistakes and faults of others that affected me, but I also see how God did something greater despite what life handed me. Despite how painfully the cut stung as I squeezed another lemon, He made whatever I went through worth something. And I wouldn't go back and exchange that pain for anything, knowing what I know now about where I am, who I am, and what His plans and purposes are for me.

If I had to pick one verse that could summarize my prayer for you as you read this book, it would be Romans 15:13. In it, Paul wrote, "May the God of hope fill you with all joy and peace as you trust in him, so that you may overflow with hope by the power of the Holy Spirit." He is the God of hope, peace, and joy. When we put our faith in Him, by the power of the Holy Spirit, we can bear these fruits in any season—anywhere, anytime, in any circumstance.

Whether you feel burdened by hopelessness, suffering, despair, or fear or are delighting in hope, joy, peace, and faith today, I hope this book fans a breath of fresh air into your lungs so that you can lift a lament or a praise to God, with expectancy that He will meet you where you are and see you through to the other side. Our journey has just begun, and I am grateful I get to walk alongside you in it, friend.

Though we may share in some similar sufferings, I also understand that I have never walked in your specific shoes. I won't pretend to know or relate to everything you have endured. But I will empathize. I will weep with you when you weep and rejoice when you rejoice. I'm hoping that throughout this book, in sharing my personal battles and breakthroughs, where wounded, sliced, and scarred hands have been healed by the One who mends our frayed fragments, stitches together our tears, and patches our pain with color and hope, that you, too, can step back and see how the tapestry of your life has come together to be a testimony of the Redeemer restoring your story.

Not only that, but I hope to reintroduce you to the tender Tailor, the salvaging Savior, who treats the bruises and stings that the lemons left behind and gives us the hope, peace, and joy to stay on course, to withstand the pricks of the needle, the tension of the threads, and the slow stitching of mending seasons together. When the tapestry is finally complete, and we switch from viewing the tangled back of the fabric to peering toward the front, we will see that what was woven together wasn't neglected or thrown together with no effort but is a detailed and divine masterpiece of love, hope, resilience, and purpose, redeemed by the hands of the Maker.

My Hardships Are Too Heavy

Like the fairy godmother creating a new gown for Cinderella out of the fabric her stepsisters tore apart, God takes our distressed pieces, stitches them back together, and patches over what's been exposed, repurposing and redeeming every inch. He transforms us from servants to daughters, from ruin to redemption, from sorrow to singing, from woe to wonder, and from trials to testimonies.

Now, maybe to you this all sounds nice, but sometimes nice doesn't feel relatable to the trials we are in, the difficulties we have, and the exhaustion we are experiencing because of the heaviness of our season. Suffering and silence may feel like your life right now. It's okay to admit that life might not feel like colorful banners flying high, fireworks popping off, and celebrations happening in the streets for the season you're in. I've been there.

Perhaps you've just arrived at the hardest situation you've yet to face. You're at the doorway of disappointment, and you're afraid to take that first step. No loads are letting up, and no divine direction from heaven is hitting your inbox. Maybe you feel left "on read" by this so-called always present Father. Maybe this book seems a little too "praise God" for you as you sit in a season of lament and tears.

Please know that this book comes from that place too. I'm not just your cheerleader standing on the sidelines hyping you up to cross the finish line; I have been writing this story and living out this hope from the middle of the valley, the bottom of the pit, and the deepest, darkest nights of my life. I have been there. I am

> He transforms us from servants to daughters, from ruin to redemption, from sorrow to singing, from woe to wonder, and from trials to testimonies.

speaking to you from those places of pain, and I am right there with you if that is where you are today.

Maybe you're asking, "Why do we suffer? How is God still good when we suffer? Can our flag still fly high when it feels like tornadoes are ripping and tearing through everything, including the fabric of hope we are weaving?" Together, we will meet in the ashes of what has felt burned, scorched, and set ablaze that we weren't ready to grieve, let go of, or go through, because that is real life.

But hope whispers a different ending. It graces us with the certainty that we have a real God who understands the realities of life and how, on some days and in some seasons, we are in desperate need of His hope, joy, and peace because everything feels like the exact opposite. So if that is you today, know that I am not here to meet you with fluff or to gloss over the struggle. I am meeting you in it, standing beside you to lift you up when you feel most weak, here to champion you to believe again that God is still good and He can still do something great in your story. It's not over yet!

The apostle Paul wrote in Philippians 1:6, from a prison cell might I add, "I am certain that God, who began the good work within you, will continue his work until it is finally finished on the day when Christ Jesus returns" (NLT). I am certain of this too. I once prayed for God to remove me from my suffering; I have now begun to pray for God to finish the good work He has started, confident that in all things, God can redeem it and repurpose it for a greater good than I could ever imagine.

In each chapter of this book, my prayer is that you'll see more and more of the fabric of hope God is sewing together in your life—that He can make a beautiful tapestry of what felt torn and useless. Friend, God is not just the author of our stories; Hebrews 12:2 reminds us that He is also the finisher of our faith (NKJV). What does this mean for you today? If you are alive and breathing, He's still stitching together the beginning and the end. His hands are still at work to repurpose what was once bad to become something beautiful. And if He can bring redemption and purpose into the different seasons and areas of my life that I thought were of no value, use, or restoration, then I am confident He can do it for you too.

Chapter 2

BLANKIES, BANNERS, AND BURDENS

As a child, there were three things I always requested from my parents: my binky, my blankie, and my bunny. This was my holy trinity before I got saved. I have photos and home videos of me marching around with a pacifier in my mouth, my stuffed animal in my hand, and my security blanket trailing behind me as I went about my day. They were especially essential to my nighttime routine. If I was missing any of those three things, it would be a long night of hissy fits and screaming. Why? I was attached to these specific items because they provided me with comfort, security, and peace. After all, on the darkest and scariest nights, isn't that what we all hope for and cling to? Comfort, security, and peace?

There was a trend on TikTok where people would show their childhood stuffed animals and blankets with a before picture and a present-day comparison. I would cackle as I'd swipe through to see teens and young adults cuddling little critters and soft baby blankets that were completely tattered, torn, washed out, and hanging on by their last limb or thread. It was hard to believe the vibrantly colored stuffed puppy once lovingly held by a two-year-old had morphed into a grayish, ratty, crusty bundle of fabric! As funny as that is, I think it is a testament to two things: how well-loved those items were and how much they went through with that child.

When I think of who God has been to me in my life—when I had dark nights, when I felt like monsters were lurking under the bed or within my closet, or when my nightmares felt a bit too real—it's clear that He has always been my security blanket. He has been the One I called out to, clutched, and confided in whenever things got too scary. After all, each of us has an inner child, and each of us who is in Christ has been adopted as God's child (Ephesians 1:5). I think it only makes sense that when we feel scared or unsafe, we cry out to our Father for help. And being the Father that He is, He rushes in to comfort us.

As a child, I had a giant quilt comforter that I loved. The designs were stitched together with flower prints and paisley patterns to make up one giant, beautiful tapestry. It was my favorite! I loved to trace the different squares, step back to take in the fullness of its intricacy, and dart my eyes among the colors and prints. In the same way, God has been my comforter who has draped Himself over me on the cold, dark nights like a weighted blanket, providing beauty and security in the face of anything the night brings. More than that, He has also stitched over every wear and tear with new patches and squares, weaving and designing a more personalized, unique, and Kirby-fied quilt that testifies to where He has stepped in and made all things new.

I'm sure you've had long, dark nights. Cold, sleepless nights. Nights when it felt like the daylight would never come or like the monsters under your bed were about to snatch you up and drag you under. As an insomniac, I know that the night can even be a time of anxiety and fear, causing you to question yet again if you'll ever get any rest or if it will be marked by tossing and turning once again.

Perhaps your long, dark night has been the anticipatory grief of an addict in your life who won't put down the bottle. Maybe your restless, sleepless night has left you struggling to make ends meet now that your husband has left you on your own to fend for yourself and the kids. Maybe the monster under your bed has been a daunting battle with anxiety and depression, and you're afraid that it will eventually get you when you aren't looking, dragging you back to the pit you've fought so hard to escape.

Everyone has a story. Everyone has a sensitive spot of suffering, grief, hurt, and discomfort. Each of our stories is unique, tailored specifically to the cultures we grew up in, the families who raised us—or should have—the communities we were surrounded by, the decisions we've made along the way, and the set of challenges we were each born with or into. We each have our own lives, and like a quilt, they are woven together by unique patches, patterns, squares, and stitches. They tell of our trials and triumphs, our highs and our lows, our failures and successes, our scars and sanctification, our breaking and becoming, and our regrets and redemption. But God!

But God is the silver lining who stitches it all together, revealing His beautiful design and destiny of redemption for each of us.

> God is the glimmer of hope that seeps through when the sun sets and the darkness tries to drown out any beacon of light to guide us.

But God is the glimmer of hope that seeps through when the sun sets and the darkness tries to drown out any beacon of light to guide us.

But God is the faithful thread that pulls us closer to Him when we feel as though our season is splitting us at the seams, tethering us to His steadfast love.

I know there are places where it feels as though life has torn us in two, where the moths have chewed the fabric through, and our stories feel like they are full of holes and hurts. But my hope is that we will begin to believe in the God who can take what was broken, burdened, tested, and tried, and weave everything together into something wonderful and worth it.

Our blankets serve not only as sources of security and comfort but also as banners of praise and testimony, declaring the incredible truth that our God reigns and can repurpose anything we would once have counted as useless scraps. He will bring us comfort and consolation as we feel and heal, but also confidence and assurance as we raise the masterpieces He is making high and proud like a banner, declaring His glory in our story.

Give God the scraps, the bits of fabric you've been dragging, and the blankets that have been chewed through and ripped up. We can trust them in the hands of our Savior, Jesus, whose own nail-pierced hands served as a gateway to our freedom so that we could have forgiveness, fellowship, and fulfillment in Him, by Him, with Him, and for Him for all our days.

From Blanket to Banner

My knowledge of soccer stems from two places: *Ted Lasso* and the Coca-Cola commercial that aired in 2010 for the FIFA World Cup in South Africa.[1] The song that aired in that commercial, "Wavin' Flag" by K'naan,[2] became iconic. That song was everywhere back in 2010! Every commercial, radio station, and school function was blasting it. From child to adult, from east to west, people would pick up a piece of fabric lying near them and wave their "flag" to the lyrics of this song, singing along at the top of their lungs. I know that we will only experience true unity and peace when Christ comes back for His church and restores our world at His second coming, but "Wavin' Flag" brought a sense of unity to the world that was second only to that.

This song's lyrics tell of the resilience, freedom, and celebration that come from endurance, struggle, and hope. K'naan knows about this firsthand, having witnessed struggle, strife, and oppression in Mogadishu, Somalia, during their civil war. Luckily, his family was able to seek refuge in Canada in his teen years and find freedom from the hardships they had witnessed and endured.[3] Not many people know about K'naan's background, and I'm sure not many people know the story you've lived to tell either. But what I know is that at some point, each of us has picked up our makeshift flags and flown them as a sign of hope, joy, and victory out of the places of pain we've personally experienced.

Waving flags is nothing new to humanity and is seen across different cultures. Even in the Bible, we read about the banners that the Israelite people made to testify about the goodness of God in the midst of their battles. They would wave these banners with confidence, declaring who these tribes and people were and, more importantly, who their God was.

Psalm 60:4 says, "But you have raised a banner for those who fear you—a rallying point in the face of attack" (NLT). During battles, banners were propped up so that the tribes would have something they could see and rally around to celebrate victories.[4] When Moses and the Israelites were fighting against the Amalekites, God instructed Moses to hold up his hands, and so long as he did, they would win the battle (Exodus 17:11). By the end of the battle, Moses was perched on a rock with two men holding up his hands from either side so they could overcome their enemies, and it was done (v. 12). Israel had won.

In honor of that, Moses and the tribes of Israel built an altar to the Lord. Exodus 17:15 recalls this, saying, "And Moses built an altar and named it, 'The LORD Is My Banner'" (CSB). The Lord is My Banner! This title for God is translated as *Jehovah Nissi*. Whenever anyone—friend or foe—would look upon the banner, they would know that the God of Israel, Yahweh Himself, had declared victory in this place and for His people. He was responsible for their triumph in the face of suffering, oppression, and battle.[5]

But this banner that was erected didn't just serve as a reminder of God's faithfulness, power, and redemption for them. It was also a symbol of God's throne, authority, and presence among His people; the banners declared that God redeems here and reigns here![6]

When I look back on the tapestry of my life and see squares of stories stitched together like a quilt, I not only gain comfort from it like I did from my favorite childhood bedspread, but I also gain confidence from it like the Israelites did with their banners. David once wrote of his confidence and hope in God (Psalm 71:5). I, too, hold on to hope and confidence in God's power and presence in my life. As I look back and trace the threads that testify to where I've been and where God showed up, it's so clear that God was always with me, calling me to look up at Him and to fix my eyes on the banner of hope He was waving, declaring, and proclaiming over my life. God is my banner; He is Jehovah Nissi to me! And He can be a banner of hope to you as well.

When you feel as though life has knocked you down with another blow on the battlefield, look up and remember who God is, what He has declared, and that the war has already been won by

Him. We can hope in what Psalm 24:7–8 worshipfully states about our God, "Lift up your heads, you gates; be lifted up, you ancient doors, that the King of glory may come in. Who is this King of glory? The LORD strong and mighty, the LORD mighty in battle." The God who holds us when we feel like we cannot get up or keep moving forward has the power and authority to see us through to the other side. Our King of glory, with arms outstretched and love poured out, died and rose from the grave so that you and I can overcome and endure every season, circumstance, situation, and suffering with joy, faith, peace, and confidence. Yes, we can cover ourselves with hope like a blanket and be comforted, secure, and safe, but we can also raise it high like a banner, having confidence, joy, and endurance to keep moving forward because the victory belongs to our God (2 Chronicles 20:15; Proverbs 21:31; Exodus 14:14).

This is not just a future hope that will be attained only upon entry at the pearly gates, my friend. This is something we can experience today. You can grab onto the fabric of hope today, whether your fabric is hanging on by a thread or beautifully sewn together, and embrace both the comfort and confidence of our God, who intervenes on our behalf. For you, it may look like grabbing hold of His garment like the woman with the issue of blood in Luke 8:43–48, clinging to His presence and power in the ever-changing seasons of life. Maybe grabbing onto the fabric of hope looks like falling to your knees in prayer and worship, even though the rain is still pouring down on you. Perhaps it looks like speaking the name of Jesus over your fear and anxiety because you know, according to

Hebrews 10:23, that He who promised is faithful to fulfill every vow He makes. For me, it looked like shifting my focus to God and remembering how much bigger He is than my present-day problems, even though they seemed all-consuming. It looked like trusting in His faithful record of redemption in my past when I was unsure how the bad news would affect my future.

Friend, I need you to know that hope isn't just a prediction; hope is a posture. One of getting low but also standing tall. It means letting the Lord cover you as you submit before Him in your desperation and then rising with confidence that He is who He says He is. Hope is a place of stability and security, one that we can stand on with assurance that as we are rooted and grounded in Him, we will not be shaken. Hope is not passive. It is active faith in the One who can do a new thing and redeem an old thing; who is neither distant nor delayed; who is presently purposing the places you've been and the place you're in right here, right now.

You Can Trust Who Knits You Together

Not only does this banner that waves high give us confidence and coat us in comfort like our favorite weighted blanket, but it also gives us clarity as to who we can always trust. You can rest in the truth of our all-powerful and present Savior when life gets hard and your burdens feel too heavy to shoulder. You can lift your eyes and remember the promises and truth of who your hope is best placed in: Jesus rules and reigns (Revelation 19:16), He has ordained your days (Psalm 139:16), and He redeems all things (Revelation 21:5). He knit you together in your mother's womb the moment you were conceived, but His plans and design for your life didn't stop there (Psalm 139:13). He has continued to sew, stitch, and weave His glory into your story.

I don't know about you, but I am not the biggest fan of needles. I remember when I got my ears pierced for my eighth birthday, I cried and fought off the teenager with the piercing gun for about an hour in front of all my friends. I was petrified of the pain that I was about to go through. You would have thought this lady was pulling out my teeth without any anesthesia, given the strength I was fighting back with. Eventually I calmed down, and after two quick pinches of pain, my earrings were set into place. I remember looking in the mirror with my bloodshot eyes and snotty nose and then seeing my gold earrings glistening. Immediately I turned to the lady, thanked her, and went on to party it up with some Hannah Montana karaoke as if my screaming and crying hadn't just happened. Every time I think back on it, I laugh, now that I am far removed from the anticipation and pain.

Similarly, God stitches things together, which means there's a needle that pulls the thread behind. A needle and thread we often dread. We want it to be over. We want the work of redemption and restoration in our lives to be pain-free and finished in an instant. Microwave miracles and Febreze faith. We want to dance around with our glittery earrings and beautiful fabrics that the Tailor's hands have mended, but sometimes there are pinches before the finished product appears.

Blankies, Banners, and Burdens

If you are in a pinch today and feel the creeping anxiety and weight of pressure looming over you, I want you to know that God isn't trying to hurt you with an ear-piercing needle. The areas that you want stitched together by Him will be graced by a tender needle carrying silver thread marked by peace, joy, and hope. I know that some of the punctures and piercings cause us pain, but His precision and placements are not tearing us apart; they're tethering us to a place of deeper healing and trust. We can yield and surrender to God, looking to Him with confidence that, just as He has carried us in every season past, He can also get us through our current situation. We also gain clarity when we look toward the future, knowing that God goes before us and He will weave whatever wounds we have into something healed and whole.

> We can yield and surrender to God, looking to Him with confidence that, just as He has carried us in every season past, He can also get us through our current situation.

Coming from a lineage of artists, I love to be creative any chance I get! There were many times in my life when I explored and expressed my artistic side through various media. The very beginning of that artistic calling looked like three-year-old me taking a Sharpie and drawing all over the walls and furniture in my house after I was inspired by my nana Marsha, who was painting my childhood bedroom at the time. Sure, to the adults it was a mess, but to little me, it was art! Since then, I've taken a shot at things such as flower arranging, clay sculpting, jewelry making, scrapbooking, and even crocheting. No walls were harmed in those creative processes, thankfully.

In high school, I attempted watercolor painting for an art project I was assigned. I took my time, trying to control the flow of the droplets and the colors to get it exactly as I wanted, but sometimes they ended up doing their own thing. They would bleed through, drip in the opposite direction, and the hues would be off. I remember ditching a few of my projects because they seemed too messy or not how I had pictured them. As I was talking to my teacher one day, showing her some of my rejects and discards, she encouraged me to go with the flow. To surrender to what was out of my control and see how it could be redeemed and repurposed into something more beautiful than what I had initially imagined. This challenged my perfectionistic, control-freak side in more ways than one—not only in my art but also in my faith.

Isn't that similar to God's presence in our lives? He meets us in the middle of the mess, the chaos, the colors that went outside the lines, and makes it into a work of art that we couldn't have ever known was possible—His heavenly handiwork! It reminds me of the fifteenth-century Japanese art form *kintsugi*. Whenever pottery was cracked, broken, or shattered, rather than discarding the pieces and labeling them all as waste, artists would instead restore it by mending and filling the cracks with urushi lacquer with gold powder.[7] The artists piecing them back together didn't just fill in the cracks and smooth over them but highlighted them and incorporated the redemption and restoration of these pieces into their story and display. They dignified each piece with the gold, adding more value and beauty than it had previously. This whole art style stems from the Japanese worldview of *wabi-sabi*, which embraces imperfections and impermanence, and the idea that brokenness doesn't dictate something's end but is simply a part of the story.[8]

Isaiah 64:8 says, "But now, O Lord, you are our Father; we are the clay, and you are our potter; we are all the work of your hand" (ESV). Each of us is a vessel carefully crafted, shaped, and smoothed out by the Lord's careful hands. But as we go through life, chips happen, cracks form, and sometimes we fall from the shelf and break. When I was in college, dealing with anxiety from an unhealthy relationship, I increasingly became chipped and cracked, and was eventually left utterly broken. Learning how this guy was living a double life—dancing at clubs with other girls and getting drunk, all the while putting on the front that he was some faithful Christian guy—wrecked me. He even confessed to me that he had lied about believing in Jesus. The deception felt like a stab in the back. I felt like a fool. I felt out of control. I didn't know what good could come from the shattered pieces I had become. I felt like parts of my heart were stolen and fractured, while other parts of my mind were cracked and fragmented.

But God didn't just sweep me up into the dustbin or toss me into the recycling. He is a wabi-sabi kind of Redeemer! One who repurposed my brokenness to serve as a testament, a mosaic, a *kintsugi* of His kindness. That is the gold that shines forth!

Looking back on my life, it is clear to me that even with my best efforts at controlling my life and keeping everything pretty and perfect, the beautiful things that have come forth were birthed out of God's divine intervention in moments of mess and madness. When I surrendered to Him and gave Him the potter's wheel, the paintbrush, and the gold lacquer, He started introducing colors, shapes, curves, and dimensions I never would have imagined. He pieced me together in a new way that felt whole. He filled in the gaps, sometimes went outside of the lines, and made the canvas of my life into an incredible mosaic of His faithfulness and plans.

If anything, I'm probably more of a mixed medium than a mosaic, consisting of all sorts of bits and pieces that I trashed and thought were unusable, only to be repurposed for something more complex yet more beautiful. Like fabric, we can be stitched back together by Him and be stronger at our seams—sharper and softer. Crazier and cleaner. Detailed with shiny silver stitches and glistening gold glazes. Here, with Him, beauty is possible.

Chapter 3

GOD IS FAIR, LIFE IS NOT

Are you ready for everything you think you know to be true about lemons to shatter before your eyes?

God did not give us lemons. We did.

Scientists claim that lemons are the hybrid result of citron and bitter oranges being spliced together through centuries of farming. They know this based on genomic sequencing. That's how we ended up with what our modern-day lemon is.[1] So I guess you could say that life didn't give us lemons. We humans gave them to ourselves! How fitting.

I know some people blame God as the cause for all of the world's problems, but it's actually the opposite. We made lemons, we gave birth to sin, and we reap the spoils of sour situations that affect us and others. But God, being so good, decided to do something about humanity's lemon problem. He added some sugar to the mix to sweeten the bitterness and brokenness of life. He redeemed its mouth-puckering punch. Throughout the biblical narrative, we see God intervene through His mercy and grace, providing opportunities for humanity to be freed from their sin, empowered to live a sanctified life, and redeemed into a right relationship with Him. Simply put, His way works!

When Your Timeline Is a Multiverse of Misery

A popular concept in TV and film right now is the idea of the multiverse. Every time we follow a character into these parallel universes where life is completely different from what they know, it can usually be traced to the character making a decision that is uncharacteristic for them, changing the whole outcome of events. There is no way these characters could know the extensive changes their choices may lead to, whether they made a decision on sheer impulse or they spent time weighing out the right options from the wrong. The lesson we can draw from this is that our decisions matter and they can lead to a variety of outcomes and endings. While we might anxiously wonder what might follow, only God, who is omniscient, knows every detail that could result from our choices: how they affect us, others, our communities, our nations, the world, our relationship with Him, and so forth.

God knows the why behind everything that has ever happened. The decisions that led to the disappointment, the falling dominoes in your path that knocked you down, and the choices others have made that have indirectly affected you. We don't know all the inner workings of what's taking place behind the scenes, but there is a ripple effect that eventually reaches us. We hope, wish, and pray that things could have end up differently, but as we know, every action has a reaction.

I know some of us see this evil, have been affected by it, and struggle to reason how on earth God could ever be good if He allowed it to happen. But just because evil exists doesn't mean a good God doesn't. I think, if anything, it points to Christ all the more and the necessary conviction we all have that the world was never meant to be this way, and that there must be something better. Spoiler alert: That something is someone, and His name is Jesus.

God knows all these things. In the divine balance of His sovereignty and our free will, God is still able to work out any outcome for a greater good. What we can't rewind, He redeems. What feels like a delay, detour, or disappointment can be woven into a greater design. But we must go to Him, entrust these hurts and hardships to Him, and lean into His restorative work.

The Good Shepherd's Perspective

We humans have a tendency to hide, shame, numb, doomscroll, binge, wallow, and hyper-fixate when we go through tough times.

We indulge our addictions, exhibit toxic behaviors, and experience hopelessness. But God is different from us, thankfully. He doesn't flee, fret, forsake, or forget about us when we decide to crash out instead of run to Him. He remains, He soothes, He draws near, and He leads us to the other end of the tunnel where light is beaming through. He doesn't see our mess and scoff at our flaws; He heals us and deals with us gently and graciously.

> He remains, He soothes, He draws near, and He leads us to the other end of the tunnel where light is beaming through.

Proverbs 14:12 says, "There is a way that seems right to a man, but its end is the way to death" (ESV). In contrast, Isaiah 55:8–9 tells us this about God, "'For my thoughts are not your thoughts, neither are your ways my ways,' declares the LORD. 'As the heavens are higher than the earth, so are my ways higher than your ways and my thoughts than your thoughts.'" When we follow God's will, way, plans, and path, we end up living in Christ's eternal life and light (Proverbs 4:18; John 8:12). He lifts us up out of the pits we've fallen into, or were pushed into, and places us in peace, joy, and hope where He dwells!

Now you might be thinking to yourself, *Okay, Kirby. If Christ brings about life and light in my life, then how come I am currently living in a reality that feels like death and darkness?* First, I want to validate everything that you're feeling. As a fellow human being who is also on this side of heaven, I know what it looks like to suffer, to sin, to be struck by the lowest of blows in life, and for it to feel overwhelming, unfair, and poorly timed. That's why I want to introduce you to Psalm 23. Let's read it together out of the English Standard Version translation:

> The LORD is my shepherd; I shall not want.
> > He makes me lie down in green pastures.
> He leads me beside still waters.
> > He restores my soul.
> He leads me in paths of righteousness
> > for his name's sake.
>
> Even though I walk through the valley of the shadow
> > of death,
> > I will fear no evil,
> for you are with me;
> > your rod and your staff,
> > they comfort me.
>
> You prepare a table before me
> > in the presence of my enemies;
> you anoint my head with oil;
> > my cup overflows.
> Surely goodness and mercy shall follow me
> > all the days of my life,
> and I shall dwell in the house of the LORD
> > forever.

I recall reading this passage in church and hearing it referenced in numerous sermons. However, I was surprised when, in my senior year of high school, my English class was assigned to read the Bible to explore various writing styles and imagery. As if English weren't my favorite class already—hello, future writer alert—I was now on cloud nine, and all my classmates knew it. Christian Kirby was about to raise her hand to take on every question the teacher asked about Psalm 23. I remember my teacher asking the class what they thought this psalm was saying when it talked about how the Lord was a Shepherd who had a rod and a staff for His sheep, a.k.a. His followers. Instead of calling on my raised hand, my teacher picked the kid who sat in the back of the classroom: the student who unapologetically hated God and therefore hated me.

The self-proclaimed atheist stated, "I think this means that God is going to whack the sheep who get out of line and beat them into submission. These sheep should be afraid of their Shepherd because He can and will hurt them if they make the Shepherd mad."

Everyone went wide-eyed and silent, including the teacher. I think I was the only one who scoffed out loud, ready to challenge this guy's thoughts. I blurted, "That's wrong. The rod was used to fight off any threats, like wolves or lions, that were going to harm the sheep. The staff was used to wrangle the sheep that had wandered or gotten stuck."

My teacher said, "That is correct, Kirby. This passage actually shows the loving nature of the Christian God and how much He actually cares for His flock, alert and ready to protect His sheep." I don't think that teacher was a Christian, and even she had the right context for this!

I can't say that I'm shocked by that one student's answer, though. He always challenged my Christian beliefs. I had created a YouTube channel around that time where I uploaded faith-based evangelism videos. He made a YouTube channel that parodied mine. Maybe he was saying those remarks about God out of spite . . . but what if that spite stemmed from a place of real belief? What if he genuinely believed that God didn't love him, didn't care to protect him, and would exercise His wrath on him if he got out of line? Did he learn this from a pastor? Did he assume this because of how his father treated him? Did culture or his community affirm that this was who God was?

I don't know. But I'll never forget showing up to youth group a few weeks after that and seeing him there with his girlfriend. Our eyes met across the room, and his grew as wide as saucers when he saw the goofy smile unfurl across my face. He ducked and hid in the crowd of people, but every time I think about him, I pray for him, hoping he has come to know the real heart of the Good Shepherd.

The Pit Is Not the End

Just before it talks about the rod and staff in verse 4 of Psalm 23, it reads, "Even though I walk through the valley of the shadow of death, I will fear no evil, for you are with me" (ESV). Let's reflect on the first two words: *Even though*. The author of this psalm, King

David, used language that acknowledges hardships will come. He wrote that even though he knew he would endure the valley of the shadow of death, he would have no fear because of the unwavering and faithful presence of God in his life. But what exactly is the valley?

According to Scripture, valleys symbolize places of hardship, trials, and dependency on God, as well as preparation and spiritual growth. The valley can seem like a lowly place, a hopeless pit at times, and even a deeply distressing season. But our Good Shepherd has not abandoned us to wander the valley by ourselves. We are protected by a good, present, and just Shepherd who goes after the wolves and lions who seek to devour His lambs. God binds up the wounds we've been dealt, places us on His shoulders, and carries us to safety and rest. Our Good Shepherd steps in to save us and preserve our lives from peril.

Jesus made it clear in John 10:10 that His mission is to bring us abundant life, not to steal, kill, or destroy us. He wants to restore what feels broken, bruised, dead, and defeated. I know that the ditch on the side of the road might feel like your grave right now, but maybe this is the place and position where God can begin resurrection, restoration, and renewal in your dry bones, bringing them to life—abundant life! And all this was made possible by Jesus' body being broken for our brokenness.

The messianic scripture Isaiah 53:5 prophesies this about Christ, "But he was pierced for our transgressions; he was crushed for our iniquities; upon him was the chastisement that brought us peace, and with his wounds we are healed" (ESV). Before you even got bruised and bent out of shape by the broken world we live in, Jesus made a way so you could have redemption woven into every season of your life. Because of this, we can rest assured and have hope today that, as our Good Shepherd, He goes before us, beside us, and behind us, carrying His rod and staff, not to harm or hurt us but to guard and guide us, His beloved sheep, through any terrain we will encounter.

The Fruit of the Valley

The valley is a place of hardship, as we just discussed, but it is also a place full of fruit. No, not just lemons but actual sweet fruitfulness for the life of the believer! Time and time again, the Bible is clear that valleys have significant spiritual symbolism. It is not a place we are placed in vain but a place of value for God's people! From the Valley of Baca, a once dry and barren place known as a weeping valley, turned into a place of springs and refreshment by God for His people (Psalm 84:5–7), to the Valley of Berakah, where God brought a miraculous victory to Jehoshaphat's army where they had expected defeat (2 Chronicles 20:26), the valleys God brings His people through are paved with purpose when He is the One leading the way. There is a pattern of preparation, testing, and dependency when it comes to God's people passing through the valleys, but that doesn't mean they are void of God's goodness and companionship. No, the valley highlights and magnifies God's presence and provision!

I know we think that the valley is the scariest place, probably because the valley of the shadow of death doesn't sound like your top bucket-list vacation destination, but it is not a place we have to fear. God provides in the valley, prepares in the valley, and purifies in the valley. We get to encounter Him in some of the most significant ways as we pass through that place. We can have hope in this because He is with us (Psalm 23:4). He is our companion (Isaiah 43:2), our comforter (Isaiah 66:13), and our covering (Psalm 32:7) no matter where we go, and this includes the valley!

Valleys, although refining, are where we get planted, tilled, pruned, and nurtured so that we have the necessary fruit for whatever mountain lies ahead. This is why they are such a vital part of the journey God is bringing us on. I get that it's not the most fun place to be, but those mountaintop moments don't last either. What does last is the fruit that endures from the valley in every season God leads us into, every battlefield He emboldens us to navigate, and every mountain He calls us to climb. Our Good Shepherd knows the best spots for His sheep to dwell and dine, whether mountain-high for a time or valley-low for a season.

Psalm 23:5 talks about this, saying that our Good Shepherd prepares a table before us in the presence of our enemies. Historically speaking, the shepherd would find the best grazing areas for their herd of sheep, essentially "preparing a table for them" to eat at that is abundant and safe. What David meant was that wherever God allows us to go and whatever valley He leads us through, He goes before us to prepare a safe place where He will provide for us. He doesn't leave us to hunger, thirst, and fear for our lives in the valleys and the shadows. He has already scouted out the land and cleared the way so we can pass through with Him to the pastures where relief, refreshment, and refuge are found.

I find it interesting that this table is in the presence of our enemies. Remember that David himself was a shepherd who did the work of preparing tables for his own flock, warding off the predators that lurked in the foliage all around. The Bible tells us that David fought off lions and bears to protect his sheep (1 Samuel 17:34–37). I'm sure, in the moment, David was scared and prayed that God would take all of that away, but to David's surprise, it was those battles that prepared him to defeat Goliath and eventually become king of Israel. God protects us from becoming prey, but He also positions us in our valleys so that we can accomplish greater things with greater purposes than we can imagine right now.

One thing God places on the table before us, His beloved sheep, is bread—daily bread. Jesus taught us to pray for this in the Lord's Prayer, found in Matthew 6:9–13, and I think it's something to take note of. Daily bread might look like us asking Him to supply us with the strength we need to keep pressing forward, even when it feels silly to hope again. Our daily bread might look like Him granting us wisdom and discernment to make hard decisions that won't just affect us but those we love too. Our daily bread might look like Him giving us peace that surpasses our understanding, a timely word of encouragement, or even the provision we believed and prayed for. Whatever sustenance He gives you for today, whether it's what you ordered or not, if He gives it to you, then it is good for you. He has our best interests in mind always and withholds no good thing from His sheep who live their lives for Him (Psalm 84:11).

The valley is a fruitful place after all. He provides us with the wisest direction, the safest protection, and the perfect daily nourishment we need to be strengthened and sustained for whatever awaits us in the valleys and mountains. But as much as you are a sheep to the Good Shepherd, you are also the beloved child of the *perfect* Parent. The love and care He has for you are unmatched by any other kind of love and care out there. Maybe you've doubted this or questioned this because of some of the valleys you've gone through, some of the lions who've lurked along the path, and even some of the pits you've heard of others falling into. I know I've heard the cries of others and how they felt abandoned to the wolves. So how do we reconcile this? How can we make sense of our Good Shepherd when there is still so much bad prowling on the sidelines and in the hearts of men? Shouldn't He do something about it?

> The love and care He has for you are unmatched by any other kind of love and care out there.

Is God the Bad Guy?

Centuries and centuries of humanity's sinful choices have soured the world we live in today—a world where spouses cheat on one another because the "spark" just isn't there anymore, and the looks and feelings have started to fade. A world where money causes corrupt politicians and business leaders to make decisions that harm innocent civilians. A world where people numb their pain through pills and pixels, trying to escape the ache of day-to-day life. A world where fast fashion leads to the exploitation of workers, and our oceans have become a cesspool of pollution. A world where children are exposed to violence, pornography, and confusing worldviews online before they can even recite their ABCs. All these unfortunate realities result from a long domino chain that links back to humanity's sinful desires, leading us to make selfish and rebellious decisions, big and small. It's simple cause and effect. Yet we look at our own brokenness, suffering, and lemons, and try to blame God for life's bitterness.

So many people view God as the enemy when they should view the Enemy as the enemy. I'm talking about Satan. He is the one who manipulates our flesh, mobilizes his demons, and misguides the world—not God. God brings peace, healing, and justice to these things, actually. He is the One who brings order and wholeness, whereas the Enemy instigates disorder and chaos. God brings resolution and redemption, whereas the Enemy plans ruin and rebellion. God brings hope and joy, whereas the Enemy breeds despair and confusion. We need to stop believing the lies and pinning the blame on the wrong person!

God Makes Right What Life Got Wrong

In many ways life feels unfair, unjust, and unkind, but God is fair, just, and kind. He makes right what went wrong! I love that we get this perspective from Job, of all people—the righteous man who suffered so greatly—who said in Job 34:12, "Truly, God will not do wrong. The Almighty will not twist justice" (NLT). God will bring justice in His perfect timing. By this, we know that He will do right by His law and by you. Deuteronomy 32:4 also proclaims, "He is the Rock; his deeds are perfect. Everything he does is just and fair. He is a faithful God who does no wrong; how just and upright he is!" (NLT). In all His ways He is righteous! This means that He will handle things rightly and not deviate from His nature. Whatever it is that He promises, and how He says He will handle things, He will follow through.

Not only is God fair, a.k.a. just, but on the same side of that coin is His mercy. I love how Psalm 85:10 shows the relationship between God's justice and His mercy, saying, "Love and faithfulness meet together; righteousness and peace kiss each other." They kiss each other. They are joined together. God is just and judges fairly, yet He also greets those who approach Him with mercy. Even when we least deserved it, He extended mercy toward us, not giving us what we deserved but rather showing us undeserved grace. Isaiah 30:18 also displays this, stating, "Therefore the LORD waits to be gracious to you, and therefore he exalts himself to show mercy to you. For the LORD is a God of justice; blessed are all those who wait for him" (ESV).

Because He is merciful, just, and compassionate, God meets us in our suffering and does something about it. He redeems what was meant for evil, turning messes into ministries and trials into testimonies. He relieves what has felt burdensome, providing peace where there was pressure, lifting the weights off us that we couldn't carry on our own. He supplies our every need, providing for us so that we lack nothing. He sustains us through every season, carrying us through the journey as a faithful companion.

Maybe you've lost everything—your job, your family, your home, your sense of purpose. God can do a new thing, open new doors, give new life, and even restore the old things that were taken from you. Perhaps you've been the girl with the long-lasting struggle with addiction, and God is giving you His strength and His supply so that you can live out real hope, real transformation, and a real testimony that will lead to the freedom and healing of others. Or to the person who felt silenced as a child, used and abused by those who were meant to be her protectors: Maybe God is restoring you in this season so you can be the voice for the voiceless, advocate for those who have nobody to call upon, and show them that real love from a kind, holy, heavenly Father does exist.

Sometimes God removes us from the suffering, and other times He redeems us out of the suffering. Either way, He shows up. He does something about it. He gives us the peace we need, the joy we need, and the hope we need to endure the valley, whether we planned to go through it or not. I have learned that He is enough, that He is good, and that He makes something out of our messes, trials, and brokenness.

As someone with a chronic illness who prays every day for God to take it away and heal me, I trust that if He doesn't heal me on this side of heaven, I will still see His hand at work in my life in miraculous ways through this suffering. I wish I were fully healed.

I wish the pain would leave in the snap of a finger. But God hasn't done it yet. Maybe He will, maybe He won't. But that won't change what is true about Him. I have assurance that if I am going through it—and so long as I invite Him into it—it won't be for nothing. He will use every season and situation for something greater than I could comprehend—for the culture, for the kingdom, and for my character.

Believe me when I say that I get it. I have been through various valleys. But I've also seen that God can do something great with your lemons if you let Him. Like a master chef on your favorite cooking show, He can use that lemon to add zest to something that once seemed dull, bland, meaningless, or worth abandoning. He can grate it into something greater, squeeze it into something of significance, press it into something purposeful, and mix it all into a masterpiece. Things may spoil and go wrong in hell's kitchen, but nothing goes to waste or is irreconcilable in God's kitchen! He is the sugar that cuts through the bitterness and sweetens the deal. He is the Redeemer who meets us in our brokenness and helps us heal.

So maybe now is the time to hand over those lemons life has dealt you into His hands. Maybe this is the season where you need to begin trusting that He can redeem the ingredients that, at one point, didn't seem to complement one another. Maybe today you need to give Him the space and grace to whip up something that is Michelin Star worthy. Let the church say, "Amen, Lord!" Let the church say, "Yes, Chef!"

Chapter 4

YOUR WOUNDS HAVE A WHY

Have you ever felt like the trial you were going through was pointless? That the suffering or sorrow you were facing was meaningless? Like this change or hardship was nothing but a waste of time and tears? I won't lie to you; I've felt that way. As much as I've been able to gain perspective on God's plans and purposes on the other side of the valley, sometimes my point of view was a bit foggy when I was in the thick of the trial, heartache, or hurt. I have openly questioned God about why He allowed me to endure specific struggles and go through certain seasons. I've pleaded with Him to let it be over with, complained to Him about how it was all for nothing, and even tried to bargain with Him to speed up the journey so I could arrive already.

Why won't You deliver me from my discomfort and discontentment, Jesus?

Why must this season go on for so long, God?

Why is this the lot in life I've been given, Lord?

Why, why, why . . . ? Those are honest prayers I've prayed, cried, written in my journals, and wrestled over with God. The whys behind these wounds were eventually resolved in my life, but not instantly.

I see this pattern throughout the Bible in the lives of people like Job, Paul, and even Jesus. Their suffering, trials, and moments that felt meaningless or miserable weren't wasted or left unredeemed. It all added up to a bigger story with greater glory. Let's start with Job.

The Wise Way to Wrestle with Our Whys

Job was known as a righteous man who honored the Lord, lived a blameless life, and had integrity (Job 1:1). Not only that, he was blessed materially, being the richest man in his area (v. 3), and relationally, having a large, loving family and friend group. Job was also devoted to the Lord in all he did, loving Him and serving Him out of the overflow of his heart. I think if we had known Job in real life, we would have all agreed that this kind of man deserved a good life and every blessing that one could receive.

But here is where Job's story gets interesting. He never did anything to bring about the chaos that was about to tear up his life like a tornado sweeping through Oklahoma's Panhandle, yet that's exactly what took place. In the spiritual realm, Satan approached God with the bold claim that Job only loved and worshiped God because of everything He had blessed Job with (vv. 9–11). I bet Satan believed that Job thought, *Life is good, so God is good! As long as He keeps blessing me, I will give Him all my devotion.* I know some people live their lives this way and base their relationship with God on this same idea, especially in our modern-day Western society, but was it true for Job? Did Job only love and worship the Lord because life was going his way?

God allowed Satan to test Job, which resulted in Job losing practically everything in his life (1:13–19; 2:7). His wealth and livestock? Gone. His servants and children? Taken away. His health? Drained. I know we've all had bad days, but this takes the cake! Job was taking hit after hit, leaving him bruised at rock bottom. This confused everyone around him. All the voices of reason in Job's life, like his wife and friends, told him to give up on God. They also started to blame Job, falsely accusing him of doing something wrong to have deserved all this (Job 4:7–8; 8:20; 11:14–15).

But in his anguish, confusion, and humanity, Job wrestled with the *why* wisely. *Why, God?* He expressed his anger, his confusion, his brokenness, and his desperation for answers, but he never blamed God (2:10). Instead of cursing Him, Job continued to praise the

Lord because He knew who God was and who God wasn't in the suffering (1:21). In his raw and real questions, his honest laments, and his deep distress (3:1–11), Job still had a confident conviction in God's just character, even though his suffering didn't make any sense.

The most compelling part of this story is that God eventually responded to Job, but not in the way we would expect. I'm sure if we were in Job's sandals, we would be anxiously anticipating some sort of explanation as to why our good God allowed us to go through all this. We, as the readers of this story who sit on the other side of it, know all the backstory and side conversations that happened, but Job didn't. And that's exactly what God didn't do: give an explanation. Answer the *why*—the very thing we'd all expect and hope for. Instead, God answered with a revelation of the *who*: who God is in the midst of our suffering as *sovereign* (Job 38–41). This left Job in awe, overcome with humility, faith, and a deeper and more real reverence for God (42:1–6).

But Job's story didn't end there. God *restored* Job and everything he lost (42:10–17). Job didn't just walk away with what he came into all this with: his friends, family, livestock, and health. He also left with a deep transformation and revelation of who God is in our suffering.

Nowadays, our society is so transactional, and I see it bleeding into our relationship with God in many ways. I especially witness it in the area of suffering. We think that good behavior warrants a blessing, and when suffering happens, either we are to blame or God is. But what can we learn from Job's story? That even the faithful face troubles. It might not make any sense to us why we are going through suffering, but what if, in it, we are granted the opportunity for an encounter with God that brings about a greater inward transformation and realization of God's sovereignty? That He is still at work. That He is still in control. That He will still meet us in that place, and we can encounter the who when we can't understand the why.

Some of my sweetest seasons have been the seasons in which I have suffered the most. Here are a few examples of the sour versus the sweet I've faced:

The sour: my mom relapsing with her alcoholism when I started high school. The sweet: giving my life to Christ just before that and having Him as an anchor of hope to cling to.

The sour: getting bullied and made fun of because I was following God's call on my life to pursue ministry and post Christian content online. The sweet: seeing thousands of people hear the gospel for the first time because of my faithfulness to post, leading others to come to faith and freedom in Jesus.

The sour: having a close friend go behind my back to secretly date my ex-boyfriend after she was the person I confided in when the breakup happened. The sweet: God mending my broken heart and introducing new friends into my life who helped walk alongside my healing from that hurt.

I know it might be hard to rationalize that there is sweetness alongside the sour, especially if you are weighed down by adversity and troubles today, but it's true. We need the who more than the why.

I'm sure you've brought many whys to the Lord: *Why did You allow me to tear my muscle and therefore lose that scholarship I was working so hard to get? Why didn't You intervene when my coworker defamed me behind my back, causing me to lose my job? Why did You place me in this dysfunctional family where I have to be the support system for everyone when I can barely stay afloat mentally and emotionally myself?*

But have you asked Him *who? Who are You when things go south, God? Lord, who do You say that You are when I get treated unfairly and my suffering doesn't make sense? Who do You reveal Yourself as in Your Word, Jesus, and how can I begin to hope in You with my story in this season of life?*

The simple answer to the why is that we live in a broken world filled with fallen people. I know we want something more explanatory, but sometimes it's more complicated than just one singular answer or reason. But what's most important is the who that comes in, picks up the fallen pieces, and lays down a foundation of restoration from what has befallen and fractured us.

A Time and Place for Glory and Grace

I went to a Christian university called Dallas Baptist University, and whenever a girl was asked who her "Bible crush" was, nine out of ten girls said Paul. I know King David cheated with another man's wife and had him murdered to cover up the illegitimate pregnancy, but I thought more girls would go for him, considering he was the poetic and heroic type. David is described as healthy and handsome, with beautiful eyes (1 Samuel 16:12 ESV)—the Bible's pretty boy! But I think it was the faith, the belief, and the joy of Paul and his unwavering dedication to the gospel that granted him so much favor in the eyes of young "sheologians" across campus.

Who is my Bible crush, you ask? Boaz, duh! This man was a provider and the redeemer of his family. He was respectful, and he honored Ruth. Maybe all the youth group sermons about finding your "Boaz" and not settling for the "bozo" really had an effect on me. All I know is, I found my Richard (more on this later), and that, in and of itself, is proof of a good and loving God!

But back to Paul. As much as we can romanticize him and his life as an apostle, Paul didn't have it easy. He encountered his fair share of suffering and wrote all about it throughout his letters to the different churches he cultivated during his ministry.

Before his gospel work began, Paul went by the name Saul. He was initially a zealous Pharisee who went around murdering Christians, trying to stomp out the fire of the good news spreading throughout Judea, Samaria, and the ends of the earth. But while journeying on the road to Damascus, he had a radical encounter with the risen Christ that left him forever changed (Acts 9:1–6). He went on to preach this truth boldly, planting churches and raising up leaders who would continue the mission Christ had commissioned all His disciples to (Matthew 28:16–20), a call we still answer today.

But Paul suffered greatly for Christ. It didn't become a life of roses, luxuries, and ease the second he started following and serving

Jesus. It became unimaginably difficult for him. He was kicked out of towns, beaten, and stoned for his preaching, imprisoned for spreading the gospel, shipwrecked and stranded while being transferred to his own death sentence, and dealt with a "thorn" in his flesh constantly (2 Corinthians 11:23–28; 12:7–8).

We are not entirely certain what this thorn in Paul's flesh was because he never identified it, but we know a few things about it. First, Paul identified this thorn as a messenger of Satan (2 Corinthians 12:7). Second, Paul explained that this thorn was given to him so he would not succumb to pride and self-exaltation (v. 7). Third, Paul pleaded with God for deliverance from this persistent affliction (v. 8). I mean, after all, Paul got to witness and partake in miraculous healings and deliverances time after time. I can see why he may have placed a similar expectation on God to move in his life with this specific difficulty. But God had a different answer than what Paul was pleading for.

Amid his suffering, God told Paul that His grace was sufficient for him and that God's power was perfected in weakness (v. 9). Murray J. Harris wrote on this, saying, "This grace of Christ (13:14) was adequate for Paul, weak as he was, precisely because divine power finds its full scope and strength only in human weakness—the greater the Christian's acknowledged weakness, the more evident Christ's enabling strength."[1] Rather than removing the pain, God reminded Paul of the *purpose*. Rather than stripping away the suffering, God supplied Paul with *supernatural strength*.

As I mentioned before, like Paul, I have a current thorn in my flesh: the messenger of debilitating, chronic migraines. One time

I had a chronic migraine that lasted for three weeks straight. And it's not just head pain; it always brings other uninvited guests, like nausea and loss of vision. I hate it. I have prayed and pleaded with the Lord many times asking that He would remove it from me, and guess what? He still hasn't.

I've had Christians tell me that if I just had more faith, God would take it away. If that phrase has ever been uttered to you, can I just say that you are not less spiritual, less faithful, or less loved by God just because the thorn in your flesh, the suffering, or the ailment hasn't been removed? I pray that one day I will be fully healed, and that you will experience the full relief and healing from your cause of pain, too. But even if not, I know that God is still good.

I am reminded of the faith of three Jewish boys in the book of Daniel, whose captive Babylonian names were Shadrach, Meshach, and Abednego. When they were about to be thrown into a fiery furnace, they knew that God had the power to spare them, but even if He did not deliver them from it, they proclaimed they would still have faith in Him (3:16–18). Whether God wills our healing or not, we can still have faith in His healing power, knowing it is not the only evidence of His favor in our lives and our faith in Him. He is still the Healer even if He doesn't remove the thorn from our flesh, because above all else, He healed us from the stain and strain of sin's separation and devastation in our lives.

If there is one thing I have learned through this suffering, it's that God's perfect plans and purposes will always prove themselves to be present in our pain. Even though I have been dealt a hand I wish I didn't have to play, and I've begged the dealer to reshuffle the cards, here is what I have come to realize: The deepest healing I've encountered wasn't physical but spiritual, which results in everlasting life and enduring peace, joy, and hope.

Suffering, in some odd kind of backward way, has been a gift to me. It's allowed me to cling tighter to Christ and appreciate the greater suffering that was the cross. My eyes move off me and this present affliction and turn to the freedom I have in Christ because of what He willingly endured on my behalf. The same was true for Paul.

There are two things that God reminded Paul of pertaining to his suffering and situation: God's grace and God's power. These things would meet him in his weakness to sustain him and perfect him. In the promise of His present grace, God was reminding Paul that even if Paul was weak, God was not. Godly grace empowers us to have endurance to keep running the race strong, knowing that nothing is wasted when it's placed in God's hands to hold! As recipients of His grace, the natural fruit of that is unending hope, unshakable joy, and undeniable peace. God's grace is sufficient because God is sufficient. He is more than enough and gives us all that we need to last long and finish strong!

> God's grace is sufficient because God is sufficient.

His grace is sufficient, and His power is perfected in moments when we are most desperate and reliant on Him. What Paul meant by this was that it's in our lowest lows that we can see the Most High clearly. It's in the desperate dependency when we go from relying on our own strength, which is so weak compared to God's, to relying on His strength. There, we get to witness God's glory shine.

Paul knew that God's power was magnified in our weaknesses and suffering, that His strength would show up and lift Paul to do what He called and purposed him to accomplish for the glory of the gospel. It refined him and fanned his faith into a flame rather than putting out his embers of endurance. John Piper wrote, "The suffering of sickness and the suffering of persecution have this in common: they are both intended by Satan for the destruction of our faith, and governed by God for the purifying of our faith."[2]

I wonder how many of us have been trying to pray away our suffering, have forsaken God because of our weaknesses, and have tried to muster our own power and strength alone, when God was giving us a beautiful opportunity to experience His power, His might, His refinement, and His strength in ways we never could have imagined. It's in moments when I need to be operating at 100 percent that I find myself humbled and reminded of my limitations, humanity, and inability. I need to rely on God and partner with Him in everything He has tasked me to accomplish.

And you know what? As much as I hope and pray that God will heal me, I have been able to experience such an incredible intimacy with Christ in my suffering that feels so deep, so personal, and so real. Nancy Leigh DeMoss once wrote, "Though my natural instinct is to wish for a life free from pain, trouble, and adversity, I am learning to welcome anything that makes me conscious of my need for Him."[3] Suffering invites us into humility, surrender, and the opportunity to see God as our mighty leader. It has been a struggle at times to let go in that way, but it is rewarding each and every time, bringing about faithful and incredible testimonies that were only possible because there was room for God to move.

From Garden to Garden

I had the pleasure and privilege of traveling to Israel back in 2018, and one of my major stops was the garden of Gethsemane. In this garden, which still exists today, Jesus prepared Himself for the cross. He prayed to the Father. He pressed into the Father. He even pleaded with the Father in deep anguish, blood dripping down His brow, asking that the Father would deliver Him from the suffering He was about to face (Luke 22:42–44). He prayed, "Father, if you are willing, please take this cup of suffering away from me. Yet I want your will to be done, not mine" (v. 42 NLT).

Have you ever prayed a prayer like that before? *God, if it's in Your will, would You please deliver me from this?* I'm sure if God had a filing cabinet of all the prayers I've prayed that sounded like that, He would have a whole department of angels sorting and filing millions of transcripts. Maybe you've faced so much misery and injustice, and all you want is for God to take this cup of suffering away from you; it tastes like anything but lemonade! Maybe you have been betrayed by a loved one, kind of like when Judas betrayed Jesus, and you feel like you are warring for your freedom all alone. Maybe you are grieving with God in the garden as your friend is in the ICU because of that overdose, and though you hope for the miraculous recovery, there is a lingering, gut-wrenching feeling that you are not ready to receive the news that's coming.

Can I remind you of something profound? God has always shown up for His people in the garden. In the very beginning with Adam and Eve, the garden was a place of perfect and present fellowship between God and His people. It was a place marked by order, peace, wholeness, and completeness. In a different garden, Jesus communed and pressed into the presence of His Father, knowing what was to come in just a few hours—I'm talking about Gethsemane. It was there that He was betrayed and abandoned by His friends, which then led to Him being tortured by His people, ending in a gruesome and humiliating death reserved for the worst criminals. This was awaiting the precious Lamb of God.

Where one garden was marked by serenity, the other garden stood for sorrow. Where one garden stood for life, another called for death. But death wasn't the end. Even in this place of sorrow and suffering, where God's presence still dwelt, the end wasn't ruin but redemption. This is good news! This is the hope that we cling to that stitches our stories together.

That same God was with me when I was throwing my graduation cap in the air after the faithful years of studying and consuming an unhealthy amount of caffeine. He was there in the joy! But He was also there in the pain when I was throwing up my lunch for the millionth time on the side of the road because yet another cluster migraine hit me out of nowhere like an eighteen-wheeler on the highway.

I remember signing the papers for this book deal, the one I had prayed and prepared for over the course of years, and God's joy and presence were so tangible in that celebration! But I also remember signing the papers at the hospital to turn off the machines that were keeping my mother's body alive after every test proved the worst to be true: She was gone. But God wasn't. His presence was present in that pain. God's presence doesn't just show up where the joy is. He is the joy. He shows up in the celebration and the sorrow, in the good days and the bad days, in the Edens and the Gethsemanes.

I'm sure you have your own seasons of contrast where, if you took a second look, you'd find the coexistence of God at work in the most unlikely of places. You'd be able to spot the silver linings in the seasons where the rejection didn't make sense. You'd realize it was God's grace and redirection. You'd be able to notice threads of God's redemption tying all things together that felt completely unraveled and undone when they chose to walk away, while you fought to stay.

> He shows up in the celebration and the sorrow, in the good days and the bad days, in the Edens and the Gethsemanes.

I want you to look back at the past seasons of your life and answer these questions: Where do you see the thread? Where was God working and weaving all along? Bringing healing where there was hurt, peace where there was pain, comfort where there was chaos, and lemonade where there were only lemons? I think you'll be surprised at just how present, purposeful, and perfect His timing was in every detail when you take that second glance from God's point of view.

From Garden, to Garden, to Garden

Did you know that in the very end of Revelation, another garden is spoken of?

Revelation 22:1–5 gives us a picture of Eden restored:

> Then the angel showed me the river of the water of life, as clear as crystal, flowing from the throne of God and of the Lamb down the middle of the great street of the city. On each side of the river stood the tree of life, bearing twelve crops of fruit, yielding its fruit every month. And the leaves of the tree are for the healing of the nations. No longer will there be any curse. The throne of God and of the Lamb will be in the city, and his servants will serve him. They will see his face, and his name will be on their foreheads. There will be no more night. They will not need the light of a lamp or the light of the sun, for the Lord God will give them light. And they will reign for ever and ever.

This is the hope of heaven. The promise God gives to each of us who calls upon His name and chooses to submit and commit our lives to Him. From garden, to garden, to garden, God is redeeming brokenness to be restored, suffering to be healed, and sorrow to be relieved.

I know some of us are stuck in Gethsemane today. We are in a place of grieving, mourning, weeping, and wailing. Suffering is present. Our friends are nowhere to be found. The night is daunting and dark. But God's presence is palpable in this place. Sometimes it looks like the unexplainable peace we feel when the anxiety acts up. It could be the random Bible verse your friend texts you in the middle of the night because the Holy Spirit woke them up on your behalf. He shows up in the small yet significant ways to show us that He has never left us and He will not forsake us (Hebrews 13:5). This is His vow to His people!

Right now we are in the in-between—where there is suffering and joy. The now and not yet. But God is present with us in all of those places. He was present with Job, Paul, and Jesus too, remember. Whether it is now, not yet, or not until glory, He is present in your story. He is working it out to mean something more. When we press into Him, we get to journey with God in the most intimate of ways, experiencing His grace and goodness firsthand. In the final garden, where rivers never run dry and the tree of life blooms, I hope we can say that the God of that garden is the same One we knew in our Gethsemane too. But until then, take a look back every now and again to count the threads of what God has woven together that you never imagined could be repurposed. Heaven is not the only place we get to hope for all things being made new. Maybe He is doing it right here, right now.

Chapter 5

WHEN GOD CHANGES YOU, NOT YOUR CIRCUMSTANCES

For most of my childhood, I wore a mask—not an N95 mask from the pandemic or one like the Greek performers wore onstage, even though I was a theater kid. As much as I loved to perform for the crowds and take my bows, I didn't quit performing once the show ended, the applause died down, and the curtains closed. My whole life felt like one big performance pretending as though everything was fine, when in reality my life felt like a giant dumpster-fire-trainwreck hybrid.

I thought that if I tapped my feet hard enough, belted the chorus loud enough, delivered my lines convincingly enough, and got the oohs, ahhs, laughs, and cries from the crowd, then my chameleon cover would provide me with another day of peace and protection. Except, it wasn't real peace. It wasn't real protection. It was, yup, a mask.

I had quite the talent for delivering my lines to my teachers, friends, teammates, family members, coaches, and everyone else in between. You might be wondering, *What was the script?* Well, it varied, but there was always one big line I could deliver on cue and cut to the next scene. It was the notorious response: "I'm fine. Everything's fine."

The mask didn't just protect me from getting real and honest about things; it also allowed me to deflect and move on to something else. Instead of telling people how horrible my mental health was because of the bullying and loneliness I was feeling, I could say those magic words, maybe point to the A+ on my report card, and everyone believed my convincing performance. It was Oscar worthy, if I do say so myself.

Rather than confessing that my home life was in shambles and that I felt unsafe and in constant anxiety about looking after my alcoholic mother, I'd recite my lines on my mark and throw in a few jokes to show that I had everything together. *Funny and talented? Surely this Kirby girl has an easygoing life to be laughing this much!*

When a past relationship was brought up and people asked

how a specific ex of mine was doing, instead of breaking down in tears over the assault I went through, I would force a smile, shrug it off, and act as though I was unbothered and untouched. I'd just readjust the mask I felt forced to wear so I could hide the shame and panic attacks I was having underneath it all. That wasn't part of the performance. I feared everyone would abandon me at intermission if they found out what happened to me. After all, others did. Why wouldn't it be the same for every other stranger sitting in the audience?

I knew the routine: Say your lines. Do your dance. Display your medals. Make them laugh. Show off the clothes. Focus on the likes. Win them with your looks. Distract, deflect, disengage. Yada yada yada...

Hmm...

You know what is interesting about that term *yāda*? In Hebrew, *yāda* actually means to know at an intimate or personal level, to care for someone, and to know them deeply.[1] But I was "yada yada yada-ing" in order for people to know an opposite reflection of who I was, what I was going through, the storms I was facing, and the pain I was in. I thought, *Nobody can know.* To be honest, I wasn't sure how to get through these things on my own: the trials, traumas, and tribulations of life. I felt completely alone in this great performance I was putting on. It was Kirby's one-woman show.

Maybe you've performed a monologue like mine, where the smile on the outside outshone the screams that were taking place on the inside. Has the anxiety, the depression, the loneliness, and the fakery of this act started to bubble up within you, and you just can't perform any longer? Maybe, like me, you so desperately want people to see what is actually taking place, but you've believed the lie that nobody can know what's really playing out behind the scenes. Why do you think that is?

What if I told you that Jesus already knows what is taking place in the wings at rehearsals and is asking you to lay down your lines and step into vulnerability? True *yāda* with Him? It wasn't until I let Jesus into my life and let Him *yāda* me that I began to experience authentic joy, genuine peace, and actual healing. He gave me the hope and endurance I needed to fight forward in every season that tried to destroy me. It wasn't always that way, obviously, but things changed when God entered the picture and I took my faith seriously—when I began to know Him, and when I allowed Him to know me.

You see, God already knew my lines. He was familiar with the intricacies of the production I was presenting and the performance I was directing. He also knew the real story that was taking place when the curtains closed: the unseen, the unsung, the untold.

With Jesus, I could finally cut the act and be real. I finally felt safe. Seen. *Known*. No glitz and glamour, no big musical numbers and costumes, no fog machines and orchestra pits. Raw, real, peeled back, and unrefined. That was how Jesus wanted me, met me, and loved me when I had no hope. When I had little to no will to live, or a thread of faith left to cling to, He came in and began a good work in my life.

In my ruin, He restored me (Psalm 23:3 ESV).
In my pit, He pursued me (Lamentations 3:55–56).

In my depression, He delivered me (Psalm 34:17–18).
In my ashes, He adorned me (Isaiah 61:3).
In my grave, He gave me life (Romans 6:4).

I treated my mask like a hedge of protection, but it was God who showed me the care, comfort, security, and shelter I needed when the battles of life commenced.

I treated my mask like defensive armor, but it was God who bestowed upon me the armor of God to fight forward in life and persevere in hope.

I treated my mask like a character I could sink into, but it was God who gave me a real identity to be rooted and grounded in.

What Keeps Us Stuck Sinking

I feel like we all have a "thing" we know way too much information about. Whether you define it as an obsession or a hobby is up to you, but we all have one, and if you don't, you probably know someone who does.

For you, it could be K-pop, World War I history, Disney movies, aquariums, *Lord of the Rings*, Nintendo games, motorcycles, turtles, the Grinch, or maybe *The Wizard of Oz*. The list of special interests could go on and on. Some obsessions or hobbies are more common than others, and one that is especially common among women for some reason is the *Titanic*. I don't know if it's because of the movie romance between Jack and Rose, who were not real historical characters, or because of the significant history behind this sinking ship. There are even museums dedicated to it in Branson, Missouri, and Pigeon Forge, Tennessee, if you're looking to book your next vacation.[2]

As you dig deeper into the lore of the *Titanic*, there is one interesting fact that strikes me: Captain Edward Smith could have prevented the ship from sinking. There are many articles that report how his failure to listen to his team's advice on the ship's pace and course, his pride in having the "unsinkable ship," and his reluctance to get help when it was needed contributed to the tragedy.[3]

Like Captain Smith, so many of us are in sinking ships but are pretending we are cruising. Can I give you permission today to break the act, to cry out to Jesus for the saving you need, and to catch the life-preserving safety ring He is begging you to latch onto? You have the green light to grab hold of Jesus and let Him be the lifeguard of your life! You can, as the saying goes, let go and let God!

Once I stopped acting like everything was fine and actually ran to Jesus with the pain, the shame, the disappointment, the confusion, the grief, and the changes that life threw onto the scene, I could keep my head above the waves and breathe. I was no longer sinking and gasping for air, treading water, fighting for my life, and trying to look put together while doing it all. I could finally rest in God, get the help and healing my heart needed, gain perspective and wisdom about my situation, and carry on in peace.

For me, this looked like getting honest with God in my prayers. I couldn't fake "fine" with Him. Once I got real and vulnerable with Him about my struggles, the areas where I couldn't hold it all together, and admitted that I was weak on my own, He began moving in my life in big ways—strengthening me, empowering me, guiding me, and healing me. To see Him move, I had to let Him in, and that required letting my guard down and taking my mask off. I started to journal my prayers, the ones riddled with pain and those marked by praise. I had to stop faking that I was fine and finally show up completely undone before the Lord.

He then prompted me to get honest with others. This second step was a bit harder for me because it meant that I had to turn on the stage lights so others could see what was hidden in the dark. This was something I also prayed about: Who were my safe people who knew me and loved me, who also knew the Lord and loved Him? It's hard to heal and grow in hope when we are stuck in isolation. This makes sense because God designed us to be in community with one another, to bear one another's burdens, just as Galatians 6:2 details.

I remember being reluctant to share my struggles for years out of fear that people would abandon me. I was convinced my traumatic wounds required me to wear a mask and manipulate people's perception of me in order to protect myself, but I quickly realized that with my godly community, I didn't have to protect myself once I let my guard down. You know why? Because God stayed, and so did the people in my life whom God highlighted to me as safe to confess to and confide my struggles, hard emotions, and problems in.

I specifically remember bottling up the secret of my mom's addiction in high school, and after one of my best friends asked me if I was all right, I accidentally let it slip that my mom's drinking was destroying me. Wide-eyed, I analyzed every movement of my friend's face to get a grasp on how much they were going to judge me, but I was met only with love, compassion, and prayer from that friend. I desperately needed the relief that washed over me after sharing the burden I had been shouldering all alone, but vulnerability was what made it possible.

I know, as much as anyone, how hard it is to be vulnerable. It can make you feel weak at times. But that is exactly the Enemy's intention, because I found that when I was honest about my brokenness and the real-life trials I was going through with my trusted people, I left empowered and strengthened. I walked away more hopeful and healed.

Finally, I had to start surrendering to the Lord. More than just voicing my concerns and bringing Him my prayers, there was an element of action He was leading me to, and it was the act of letting go—letting go of the control, the bitterness, the timelines, the expectations, and even my attempts to fix everything and make it all appear perfect to onlookers.

I want you to think about what you need to surrender to the Lord today. Maybe it's the shame. Maybe it's the struggle and striving of trying to piece together what feels broken without any help. Maybe it's the performance of "I'm fine" and appearing as if you're strong enough on your own. You can only grab hold of the life preserver He is throwing to you if you let go of the things tying you to the sinking ships of depression, panic, hopelessness, anxiety, annoyance, overwhelm, discouragement, and anger.

Maybe it's time you surrender your need to be in charge of everything, or the resentment you have toward that person who never apologized for their actions, or the lie that you have to keep it all together for the sake of everyone else's perception of you and peace in their lives. Letting go and letting God is more than just giving something up; it's giving something over to the Captain of our souls! We don't have to try to captain our own boat and navigate a field of icebergs in a vast, dark ocean in the middle of the night. We can let God take the reins on this. But if we do hit something that's floating out at sea or get some water in our boats, we don't have to capsize either. Surrender, humility, trust, and a rooted identity will save your sinking ship; you just have to be willing and ready to let go and start letting God be God.

> Surrender, humility, trust, and a rooted identity will save your sinking ship; you just have to be willing and ready to let go and start letting God be God.

Highs, Lows, Famines, and Foes

In 2018 Hillsong Young & Free released their song "Highs and Lows."[4] This has been one of those go-to songs for me whenever I have felt tossed and turned by the waves of life or when hilltops turned into unexpected valleys. It's that one "shower song" for me that I cry my eyes out to and that one "car song" that I sing with my whole chest. It is a *good* song. If you've never listened to this song before, I encourage you to take the next five minutes and fifty-four seconds to posture yourself before the Lord and listen to it. I can wait. This book isn't going anywhere.

Okay, if you did take a few moments to play it, know that I paused from writing this to listen to the song with you, and man, I feel like every memory just rushed back to me of when that song was the anthem of my soul. My mom was in the thick of her relapse, my chronic migraines were getting more and more debilitating, and I was working with my counselor on overcoming shame and trauma from the assault I went through. I'm tearing up right now just thinking about that season of my life—not just because I remember the hurt, the heartbreak, the confusion, and the chaos of these moments and memories that felt so out of my control but because God is *so good* and redeemed every single ache and break. He is too good to let me go, just like the song says.

That song went triple platinum in my house. I would shout the words to remind and refresh my soul about the truth of who God was despite what my suffering and storms led me to feel. I sang those beautifully true words, yes, but if I am being 100 percent real with you, my prayers during that season sounded more like, *Why, God? Why can't You just heal my mother from her addiction? Why can't You just take away all my migraine pain or at least give me a clear diagnosis as to what is going on in my head? Why did that guy have to betray my trust, and now I'm left carrying the pain and shame of what I didn't sign up for?* I wanted answers. I wanted a resolution. I wanted it to be over, dealt with, done.

It was easy to praise and to believe that God was good all the time when life felt easy and when my problems were solved. However, more often than not, God did not change the situation. At least, not in the way or timeline I had hoped, petitioned, or prayed for. Instead, He changed other things . . . mainly one thing—*me*.

From the Pit to the Palace

God changed everything about me—my heart, mind, perspective, prayers, actions, attitude, and more. Not because He didn't like those things about me or that the circumstances and suffering didn't matter as much to Him as they did to me, but because sometimes God uses what the Enemy intended for evil and repurposes it for good—our good.

Maybe you've heard that saying before, but do you know where it comes from? Not the Psalms. Not Philippians. Not the Gospels. *Genesis.* It comes out of Genesis 50:20 and specifically reads, "You intended to harm me, but God intended it for good to accomplish what is now being done, the saving of many lives." Joseph said this, the favorite son of Jacob who was sold into slavery by his jealous brothers, falsely accused by Potiphar's wife for coming after her, and imprisoned and forgotten about. But in a strange turn of events (*cough, cough,* God's plans and divine direction), Joseph was eventually appointed as ruler over Egypt, saved the nation from famine, and was reconciled with his family.

Just before that reconciliation happened, though, Joseph's brothers began to worry that he might have held a grudge against them for everything they put him through. After all, they did sell him into slavery. Being the sneaky guys they were, they forged a letter on behalf of their deceased father that said, "'This is what you are to say to Joseph: I ask you to forgive your brothers the sins and the wrongs they committed in treating you so badly.' Now please forgive the sins of the servants of the God of your father" (Genesis 50:17). They wanted to make sure this family reunion ended in their favor.

But when Joseph received this fake letter, which he quickly saw through, he wept. He then responded to his brothers, saying, "'Don't be afraid. Am I in the place of God? You intended to harm me, but God intended it for good to accomplish what is now being done, the saving of many lives. So then, don't be afraid. I will provide for you and your children.' And he reassured them and spoke kindly to them" (vv. 19–21).

I bet many of you would hold a grudge against someone, especially a family member, who hated you, sold you into slavery, lied to your parents that you had died, and continuously schemed against you for their own benefit. That is some Bravo network–type drama if you ask me. Joseph could have easily held a grudge and played the judge, but he dealt mercifully with them, spoke kindly to them, and showed them an abundance of compassion and hospitality. I'm not saying I'd ever pick a favorite child, but I'm starting to see why Jacob gave Joseph the coat of many colors and took the other brothers to the Canaan Salvation Army for their back-to-school shopping.

It's easy to read this and limit it to just a Bible story, but this was a real man's real life. I'm sure that Joseph would have been belting out "Highs & Lows" from the prison cell had that song existed then. Just as the lyrics of that song express, God's hand was over Joseph's life, faithfully with him through it all, showing him mercy in every season and bringing about divine purpose from the pit to the palace.

Whether we have fallen into a pit because of our own bad decisions or been thrown into a pit by the harsh hands of a broken world and its people, God sees us and is with us. We can yield to God in the pitfalls of life, knowing He can purpose it toward a palace position, not just for our own benefit but even for the blessing of others.

There are two beautiful things about pits. First, when you hit rock bottom, the only way is up. Second, we know who the Rock is who meets us at the bottom. No, not Dwayne Johnson. I'm talking about the Rock on which we stand, which is a firm foundation for our faith to flourish.

Psalm 18:2 says, "The Lord is my rock and my fortress and my deliverer, my God, my rock, in whom I take refuge, my shield, and the horn of my salvation, my stronghold" (ESV).

The apostle Paul specifically identified Jesus in 1 Corinthians 10:4 as the Rock who was ever-present, always sustaining Israel as they went about their wilderness seasons.

From our own dry spells of desert wandering, to our restful sabbaths in God-ordained oases, Christ is the Rock who sustains us. He is the foundation of our faith, the source of our spiritual sustenance, our refuge and fortress, and our salvation and strength.

Like Ephesians 2:20 testifies, Christ is the cornerstone that holds all things together. Without Him, we would simply crumble and cave in.

As we read through the life of Joseph in Genesis, there is a common thread of God's faithful presence, stitching and weaving Joseph together into a healed, whole, and humble man. God was with him through it all, and we see so much of this throughout the final chapters of Genesis. Whether Joseph danced on the heights of the palace or made his bed among the depths of the pit, God's mercy awaited Him in every place. In the end, what was meant for evil was redeemed for good.

> He is the foundation of our faith, the source of our spiritual sustenance, our refuge and fortress, and our salvation and strength.

God Is Good All the Time...

And all the time, God is good! Surely you know that call and response if you grew up in the church, especially down here in the South where I'm from. There's even a song that popped off on social media by Forrest Frank where that is the chorus.[5] But how many of us say this out of habit rather than from the heart?

When I look at what Joseph said in Genesis 50:20, I know it came from the heart. He genuinely believed that God worked evil into an agent for the healing, intervention, and redemption of a whole nation. If He did it for Joseph, and if He is still the same God, why wouldn't He be able to repurpose the wrongs in our lives to be made right? To be good?

If you are a "back porcher" and listen to *Lisa Harper's Back Porch Theology* podcast, then you might be familiar with her frequent collaborator Dr. Jim Howard. One evening, my friend John Michael and I were sitting outside talking about theology with Dr. Howard and his wife, and the topic of God's goodness was brought into question. *Is God really good?* We all concluded that He is. I feel like that's a no-brainer, right? However, as you may know, sometimes we go through difficult times, like Joseph, that cause us to question whether God is truly good after all. I mean, why on earth would a good God allow us to go through things we consider bad?

I reasoned earlier in the book that it's not just about *why* God would allow this kind of suffering. We know we live in a broken world where people have used their free will to serve their own motives rather than the good, pleasing, and perfect will of God. Look at Joseph's brothers as a prime example. We have also reasoned about *what* God is able to do through the suffering, situations, and seasons He allows us to go through that show Him to be so good.

God is the One *who* is good, as you and I discussed earlier in Job's story, but Joseph's story points to *what* good can come out of these hard places. Maybe the pitfalls don't disprove God's goodness but reposition us to see God's goodness revealed in a greater way than we would have expected. That humbled, low vantage point gives us a whole new perspective where we get to see God stitching and threading our life's tapestry from the back. Here, it might look like a bunch of loose threads and random knots, but the front of it testifies that God was always creating something far more marvelous than we could have ever hoped for, prayed for, or imagined.

It wasn't just about the *places* in Joseph's story. It was about the *person* Joseph was throughout his story. I get that sometimes we need to pull over onto the side of the road and have a good cry. The potholes are getting the best of us, the road ragers are freaking us out, and the directions keep recalculating; it's all just frustrating the mess out of us! It's okay to feel all those feelings and bring them before the Lord. What's not okay is to make the pit your dwelling place. We are not meant to live in the pit. Joseph sure didn't.

Joseph trusted in the goodness, glory, plans, and purposes of God instead of changing the address on his license to "The Pit." He humbled himself and gave God control. He believed that good could come out of the bad because he served a good God. He allowed God to change Him before His surroundings ever changed, which, in God's perfect timing and by His grace, they did.

When we let God into the picture, what could have otherwise destroyed us or defined us for our whole lives can be used for divine destinies. That pit you are in could be the very place that gets your feet grounded on the Rock of Christ so that you can firmly stand in your divine destiny and be a part of the good that God wants to do in the world, not just your life alone. You can be an ambassador and usher of heavenly hope! Joseph's life was redeemed for good, yes, but so was the whole nation of Egypt and eventually the people of Israel too. The Enemy was after Joseph, but God redeemed Joseph and many more through the twists and turns of his journey, a journey that ultimately prepared him for the palace God had destined him to one day rule.

God redeems our pain for our own sakes, yes, but He also uses the places we've been for the good of others. Nothing is ever wasted, and nothing is ever in vain when God is invited into the story. Where you are today doesn't have to be forsaken, forgotten, or futile. It can be a place of surrender, strengthening, and sanctification. When we surrender to a life of faith, the goodness of God will break through and bring breakthrough! When we choose to let go and trust the story that God is authoring with our lives, real change happens and real hope flourishes—within us and throughout our world.

Chapter 6

FAITH WITHIN THE FABRIC

There are two types of people in the world: those who are on time and those who interpret "five more minutes" as fifteen to thirty more minutes. Respectfully, if you are in the second category, you are the worst type of person. I'm joking—clearly, God has some refining to do in my life in the patience department. And I'm sure He has some refining to do in those people who think five minutes is the same as thirty minutes.

Here is how I'm wired: I love to leave right on time so I can arrive right on time—and by right on time, I mean five to ten minutes *early*.

Listen, I have no hatred in my heart toward people who are going with the flow and living life at a slow pace. I love to do that . . . when I'm on vacation and have "slow time" penciled into my schedule. But other than that allotted time for "doing nothing," that's when I get all frazzled, frustrated, and frantic. Judge me all you want, but I know some type A person out there is shouting, "Amen!" to that.

As much as my friends and family are probably annoyed by this trait, I can only imagine how many complaints God has heard from me about *His* perfect and sovereign timing. If we are peeling back the layers here, my struggle with being patient runs deep. It boils down to issues of trust, selfishness, letting go of control, and surrendering to God's will. My version of "on time" when it comes to God is better written as "my time," if I'm honest. I have had to slow down, get before the cross, and surrender my expectations and schedule to God's timing. Truth be told, I am still being refined in this. There is a spot right next to me if you need to pull up a chair and allow the Holy Spirit to produce patience in your heart too.

Whenever I have found myself spiraling, obsessing over, or hyper-fixating on anything, my husband has been someone who has brought me back down to earth, reminding me that God is in control and that I need to ask the Holy Spirit for faith and patience. I am so thankful for him in this way because he always does it truthfully and lovingly.

The more I go through this refining process, the more I realize that faith and patience go hand in hand. One recent example of this was when God answered my prayers about going to Asia. After meeting a pastor from Japan in 2023, I felt a deep conviction to start praying that God would open a door for me to go to Asia, specifically Japan or South Korea. Could I have just booked the tickets right then and gone into debt? You bet. But that would have been irresponsible and not on God's timeline. I prayed and prayed for months on end. My husband and I often discussed this conviction that I had to go there, and he continually encouraged me that God would open a door in His perfect timing; I just needed to be patient and have faith.

So I waited. And I patiently prayed. Then the funniest thing happened, and by *funny*, I mean God-ordained. Nearly a year to the date that I felt that conviction in 2023, I got a random email in my inbox from an organization I had never heard of, saying that this was their "final email check-in to see if I still wanted my spot in Korea."

Huh? Surely this is a scam or something...

I spent a couple of hours researching this organization, made a few phone calls to some of my global mission friends, and realized that this was the Lausanne Movement, and I was being invited to the Fourth Lausanne Congress gathering in Incheon, South Korea! They had been sending me emails for the entire year while I was waiting and praying, yet every message went to the spam folder except for this one. I don't know how on earth I missed seeing those other ones, or how this one got past the spam filter, but I know God allowed me to see it at the perfect time, because it was in the waiting and the praying that He began developing trust and patience in me.

When I realized that I had been invited to this gathering that basically happens once in a generation, I praised the Lord that my prayers had been answered! Look at God, His timing, and His ways! But there was just one super important factor I couldn't overlook: It was four weeks away, and every single hotel in Incheon had been booked for months, with thousands of attendees showing up from over two hundred nations. This was when I began to panic. This was when the faith and patience that had just been developed in me were thrown out the window.

I gave them my yes and booked my flight with every airline mile I had on hand, but I had nowhere to rest my head at night. The anxiety quickly started to take over. My husband saw me slowly descend into madness as I made every call I could to friends, to hotels, to people who "knew a guy in Korea" who might help me out—but there was nothing. I got nowhere in my search for lodging. I'll never forget my husband stopping me and saying: "God called you to go. He is going to give you a room. I believe it." You'd think I, the evangelist, would have had that kind of faith and trust to believe that the God who gave me this specific conviction, call, and perfectly timed opportunity would provide for me in this moment, but nope. Here was Kirby's humanity kicking in.

I felt like the disciples when they were in the boat with Jesus, complaining about not having any food, even though just minutes before, Jesus had performed a miracle in which He fed over four thousand people. They had witnessed this miracle, got in a boat to cross the lake to their next destination, and they realized that they had only one loaf of bread to share among all of them. Cue the complaining, the worrying, the faithlessness, and the forgetfulness. Let's read what happened in Mark 8:17–21:

> Aware of their discussion, Jesus asked them: "Why are you talking about having no bread? Do you still not see or understand? Are your hearts hardened? Do you have eyes but fail to see, and ears but fail to hear? And don't you remember? When I broke the five loaves for the five thousand, how many basketfuls of pieces did you pick up?"
>
> "Twelve," they replied.
>
> "And when I broke the seven loaves for the four thousand, how many basketfuls of pieces did you pick up?"
>
> They answered, "Seven."
>
> He said to them, "Do you still not understand?"

Like them, here I was, patiently waiting on God to move in a way I believed He had revealed He would move, act, and provide—and He did! He opened the door for me to go to Korea. But when it came to waiting and being patient on hearing back from people, including the organization, about whether I would have accommodations, I immediately became frantic and faithless. I tried to figure everything out without trusting and submitting it to the Lord, my Provider, first. You know, the One who made this whole thing possible to begin with.

Guess what? Seriously, you'll never guess. God provided. No surprise there. I was offered free accommodations, thanks to the

Lord and the generosity of some donors who wanted to sponsor my stay. The only catch? I was going to have a random roommate.

I was a little anxious about this at first since I was going to a foreign country alone, on the opposite side of the world, and rooming with a total stranger. Still, as God's will and timing would have it, I ended up with the kindest roommate I ever could have imagined. Her name was Yukari, and guess where she was from? Japan!

Remember how this all started because I was praying that God would open a door to Japan and Korea for me? God delivered both in His perfect timing. Had I not been patient, had I run with my frantic spiraling rather than wait on God in faith, I probably would have wasted time, energy, resources, opportunities, and assignments by acting on my impulses rather than trusting God's perfect timing and will. Had I tried to rush it and make things happen on my time instead of on God's time, I wouldn't have connected with the people I connected with. I also wouldn't have been ministered to by the incredible people who were at this event. I now have friends in ministry whom I hope to visit in countries such as Japan, South Africa, India, Pakistan, the UAE, Switzerland, Kenya, and many more.

Patience is directly tied to knowing and trusting in God's sovereignty, timing, and plans, whether we face good or evil, the known or the unknown. We can have faith in God because He is a faithful God! Whenever He specifically calls us to something, somewhere, or someone, we can live peaceably and patiently, knowing He will open the right doors at the right time. As much as patience is about waiting *on* something, it's also about waiting *through* something. It's about enduring for the long haul with full trust in Christ.

Trusting Through the Tears

Patience is a slow process, and faith is a lifelong journey of trust. Maybe trust has been a bit of a battle for you because people have made it hard for you to trust. Maybe the circumstances of suffering have even made it hard to put your faith in God. I've been there too. But God's faithfulness isn't contingent on the behaviors of others, and neither is it discredited when God doesn't act in alignment with our expectations or timeline. He is faithful. Period. He *is*. It is a part of His divine DNA. It is displayed in all He does and through all He redeems.

God has still been faithful to me even in the prayers I prayed that never were answered the way I had hoped. When my mom relapsed right after I became a Christian, I truly felt as though God gave me a supernatural degree of patience and compassion for my mother. Not only that, I believe He gifted me a great deal of faith in Him as well: faith that He would be with me on the hard days and that He would also be with my mom in ways I couldn't. After all, Jesus is the Savior, not you and not me.

> Jesus is the Savior, not you and not me.

If you have an addict in your family, you know just how taxing it can be to have patience with them, both in their relapses and in their recovery journeys. Sometimes it can be hard to hang onto faith in times like this. It seems as though many of my family members' patience ran thin with my mom after a few relapses. Some of them were quick to judge her, quick to cast shame and blame, and quick to distance themselves from the issue when it became too much for them.

I don't blame them. I understand how hard it is to see someone choose a path of destruction over and over again, even with all the complexities and nuances that addiction carries. Setting those boundaries is necessary but also confusing. I have spent my fair share of time in the counselor's office figuring out the balance between the two: loving and supporting my mother in her healing but also not making it my specific problem to shoulder alone. Did she upset me when she was in that state of mind? Yes. It hurt. But seeing her hurt made my heart hurt more than the empty promises, the broken trust, and the disappointing letdowns. She was numbing and masking her pain.

Through this, God gave me a glimpse of His point of view. I didn't just see an alcoholic; I saw a wounded child who was numbing her pain. I saw a single mother whose trauma and trials were too much for her to bear on her own. I saw the daughter and the wife who faced so much abuse and couldn't see her own worth. My heart was shattered for her. I felt compassion for her—the same kind of compassion that God has for us and the suffering our sin and struggle causes us. When I began to see my mom in that light and have godly patience for her, *that* fueled my ability to be a witness of

Christ's love in her life. That action was proof beyond words that God was present, willing, and able to redeem and restore her from her brokenness. Although she battled this addiction until the end of her life, she came to know the real, true God of compassion, grace, patience, love, and faithfulness out of the small sliver I, a broken human myself, could extend, thanks to the Holy Spirit's power.

I'm not sure if you have people in your life who are hard to love, who have broken your trust, and who have worn out your patience, but can I encourage you that the same God who sees you, knows you, and loves you can also heal their hurt, redeem those relationships, and bind up those wounds? It is hard to surrender our loved ones who are hurting, and also hurting us through their bad choices, into the Lord's hands, but His hands are safe. He will carry them and all the while hold you too. The pressure is off you, friend. You don't have to hold it all together, or them all together, anymore. God's got this. God's got them. And God's got you.

He Weaves Together What's Been Torn

May 18, 2023, was the day the fabric of my faith was torn in two. But I must back up the timeline to paint the full picture of this massive, unexpected plummet. Just one week earlier, the tapestry of my life was like a banner flowing in the wind. The colors were caught by the sun's rays, reflecting God's promises, fulfillment, and joy in my life. Hues of pinks, oranges, and yellows danced across my face as I hit Submit on my last grad school assignment, closed my laptop, and let out a big sigh of relief, knowing that I was finally done with my master's program. I was going to walk the stage that Friday, May 12, and celebrate with my loved ones this incredible accomplishment God had called me to. All the sleepless nights, long study sessions, and last-minute cramming were worth it, including the midterm paper I had to finish writing on my wedding night (my professor gave me a 100 for that assignment). Not the most ideal time to write a paper on the early church fathers, am I right?

My mom couldn't make it to my graduation, unfortunately, because she had been admitted to the hospital a few days earlier due to a fall. It turned out they'd botched her surgery, and there was some internal bleeding, so they had to schedule her for another emergency surgery before I walked. Luckily, my husband and brother were able to come show their support and film it so that she could see her baby girl get that degree! I know she was so proud.

Just a couple of days after that, May 14, was Mother's Day. I tried calling my mom to see if she was okay and what time she wanted me to swing by the hospital to see her, but there was no answer. I assumed she was resting from the surgery because when I called her after my graduation, she was completely out of it. Little did I know that it wasn't just the surgery or drugs they had her on that had her talking all weird and not making any sense; her body had gone into sepsis, and nobody had caught it.

The following morning, May 15, I got the phone call that changed my life forever—the phone call that shredded my tapestry, which had once been flying high, bringing it to half-mast. After working at a coffee shop all morning, planning this new season of life postgrad with my first book on the way, I went home to eat some lunch but was interrupted by a phone call. I picked it up, and the person on the other end of the line asked, "Are you the decision-maker?"

My heart sank to the bottom of my stomach. All I could utter was, "What is going on?"

They replied, "Your mother is dying. You need to get here right now. She is in the ICU and it doesn't look like she is going to make it. Are you the decision-maker?" Their voice was serious and frantic. It was like a song had been set on fast-forward.

I told them, "Yes. I am. I'm on my way." I stepped out of my office, locked eyes with my husband as he was eating our lunch, and told him, "My . . . my mom is dying. We need to go!" We dropped everything and sped as fast as we could to the hospital. Angels must have been surrounding us because I know we deserved a ticket for that.

I ran into the ICU, found the floor my mom was on, and burst into her room. She was hooked up to all sorts of machines, with all sorts of sounds and alarms going off every second. I had never seen her look so bad in my life. She had a few ICU scares in the past because of her alcoholism, so part of me was holding on to hope that she would pull through yet again by God's grace, but for some reason, this time, I knew. I just knew. It was like God gave me a certain kind of grace and discernment to begin accepting what was happening, even though the medical staff was running every test they could to get a read on this situation. Over the course of three days of tests, the results came back: She was brain-dead. It was such a weird reality to sit with. Here lay my mother's body, but a significant part of her was gone.

But backing up to those three days of tests and waiting, I had my entire community of people praying for her healing. Praying that this would be the final wake-up call, the final miracle that would bring her back to life and take away the addiction. I hoped, prayed, and pleaded with God, but on the other hand, I had begun to make peace with the fact that God was calling her home.

You know how when you have a bad day you pray for God to give you a word, and you hope you turn to a Bible verse that is specific and encouraging to the situation you are in? That was me. But instead of flipping to the passages that talked about Jesus raising the dead girl back to life (Mark 5:21–43) or God being our healer (Psalm 41:3), I instead kept being led by the Holy Spirit to verses like Psalm 34:18 which says, "The LORD is close to the brokenhearted and saves those who are crushed in spirit." Or John 16:22, which says, "Now is your time of grief, but I will see you again and you will rejoice, and no one will take away your joy."

The morning that my mother took her first steps in heaven was when I just so happened to read Psalm 121. I was chronologically reading through the Psalms as a part of my own personal Bible study, and I decided I was done turning to random pages and hoping for a sign or verse from God. Ironically, that's what ended up happening. Based on the diagnosis she had received, I woke up that morning knowing that she was going to be taken off life support. The DNR she had drafted when she was alive made it a bit easier, but part of me was overwhelmed with the idea of turning off the machines that were supporting her body, even though there were no viable signs of life. God knew what He was doing with Psalm 121 and the timeline in which I was studying the Psalms, because it reads:

> I lift up my eyes to the hills.
>> From where does my help come?
> My help comes from the LORD,
>> who made heaven and earth.
> He will not let your foot be moved;
>> he who keeps you will not slumber.
> Behold, he who keeps Israel
>> will neither slumber nor sleep.
> The LORD is your keeper;
>> the LORD is your shade on your right hand.
> The sun shall not strike you by day,
>> nor the moon by night.
> The LORD will keep you from all evil;
>> he will keep your life.
> The LORD will keep
>> your going out and your coming in
>> from this time forth and forevermore. (ESV)

He spoke to me so clearly, that just as He is my keeper—in my coming and my going, sustaining my life and showing up as my helper—He was also the keeper of my mom's life, and He was calling her home to keep her safe. I needed to read that passage that morning, and God knew it. I needed that assurance and hope.

I grieved, and I am still grieving, the death of my mother heavily. To be a twenty-something-year-old girl with no parents, but especially without her mom, is strange. To think I may one day, by God's grace, be a mother, and yet lack the presence of my own wrecks me. A sable cloud of gray floats above me and rains over me as I imagine the questions I'll have with no mother to turn to and the loneliness I will feel when she is not there for those milestone moments and hard days. But the silver lining that borders that sable cloud is the truth that my God, my keeper, will be there for me. That I will never be alone. That He will provide for me the community of mothers that I'll need to uplift me as I navigate the nuances of a new season without the one person I wish could hold my hand and guide me through it.

I've had people ask me how on earth I was able to go through the trenches of my grief with real hope, not a fake smile. I think it's because, by God's grace, my mother came to know Jesus through me. I was able to cling to that great assurance the whole way through that season. God's whispers of grace, the truths in His Word, the support of my community, and the joy of her salvation in Him tended to what was torn within me. Though it was raining and pouring in my life, I could still put on my sparkly, glittery rain boots and dance in His promises and goodness where there was still mourning. God was redeeming this hurt for hope and was showing me how His goodness was present in the grief. Only God could do that.

Redemption has been all over this story and season of my life, and my hope for you is that, if you are in that trench alongside me today, sitting with your grief, loss, disappointment, diagnosis, or whatever else, you will be able to remember God's personhood, promises, patterns, and presence even when what you're seeing and feeling right now doesn't feel good or as though it could be repurposed for good. That He is bigger, better, and working behind the scenes already to make all things new.

God's redemption in this part of my story looked like finding real peace when I never thought the tears would stop flowing. It looked like a whole community of people online witnessing my grief journey and actually finding hope and faith in Christ. It looked like Him unlocking deeper empathy within me and a whole new heart for ministering to others who are mourning. But maybe for you, the silver lining of God's redemption looks like a relationship being reconciled that you were ready to give up on. Or maybe it looks like God allowing one dream to die so that a new one—a better one—can take root and bear fruit in your life and the lives of others. Or maybe it's God birthing a ministry out of something painful and long-lasting that will give life to those who thought they had no reason to keep going.

> He is bigger, better, and working behind the scenes already to make all things new.

Our Lord redeems. I know I keep repeating this, but it's because it is true. It's my favorite thing about Him! And I can't wait to see how complementary our fabrics of hope will look as they fly high next to one another once He's done stitching and sewing through our difficult seasons. They will be patched to perfection, mended into a magnificent work of art, testifying to the truth that we can hold on to hope as He keeps threading our stories to completion.

Let Christ Hold the Tension

I understand how tiring it can be to stand firm in faith. I understand how exhausting it can be to patiently and steadfastly wait on the Lord. I understand how sometimes our human tendency is to rush and to forsake God's timeline and try to take over, but can I encourage you to wait on the Lord? To hold on to faith and stand still on His promises? To be at peace and not get ahead of yourself or God?

Psalm 27:14 words it rather simply, "Wait for the Lord; be strong, and let your heart take courage; wait for the Lord!" (ESV). In Artur Weiser's commentary on the Psalms, he wrote this about Psalm 27:14 specifically: "Here faith is the power which enables the faithful to endure the tension between his present afflictions and his future deliverance from those afflictions."[1] Tension exists within life—the in-between, the famous "now and not yet." It is a present reality for many of us. Maybe you have not yet been healed. You have not yet been delivered from a really difficult season at work or in school. You have not yet been removed from that toxic household or roommate situation. You have not yet worked through the mental toll of trauma from your childhood. That doesn't have to destroy us. Our fabric doesn't have to lie scattered about in pieces of what once was. In the hands of the Healer, we can hope that it will become something again—something beautiful, testifying, and tethered, stronger than ever to weather the weather. Many of us sit hoping for the not-yet to get here already, but I'm sure if we looked long enough and remembered the goodness and truthfulness of who our God is, we would also have hope for the now we are currently in.

Right now, we have a present Helper in times of trouble (Psalm 46:1), a Savior who is near to the brokenhearted and crushed in spirit (Psalm 34:18), a Comforter who tends to our every affliction (2 Corinthians 1:3–4), a Prince of Peace who meets us when life doesn't make sense (Isaiah 9:6; Philippians 4:7), a Provider who shepherds us toward safety (Psalm 23), a Supplier of endless grace and power in our weakness (2 Corinthians 12:9), and a faithful Lord whose compassion and love never runs out (Lamentations 3:22–23).

Not only does God remain, but He also sustains. He is the bridge between what is the reality of today and the promises of what will one day come. Tension doesn't have to be a bad thing. When we reframe it through the lens of Christ, with Christ at the center, we realize this holy tension can hold us up and hold us together.

So let me ask you this: Where do you need to wait on the Lord today? Where do you need to place your faith in God today? Where do you need to invite Christ in today to hold the tension of now and not yet? I know there might be a storm swirling around you, completely engulfing every aspect of your life, and the last thing you have time for is stillness, but when we are able to get still before the Lord, surrendering a moment in time to meditate on who He is as the Author and Finisher of our faith, that time is not wasted. It is rewarded—rewarded with the peace you need to keep moving forward without worry, the joy you need to keep enduring, the assurance you need to believe for tomorrow's blessings, and the hope you need to make it to serene shores. Remember the truth, and your faith will be firmly fashioned, leaving no loose threads to be further unwoven and undone.

Chapter 7

WHEN GOD'S WILL DOESN'T GO YOUR WAY

One of my best friends in the world is Hannah. Hannah and I met while she was touring my university campus after a morning chapel session. Who would have thought that our brief run-in at the DBU chapel would eventually lead us to become classmates, friends, roommates, and sisters for life? She and I are truly cut from the same cloth! We would watch *America's Next Top Model* together, play *Mario Party* together—we even raised pet snails together in our shared room. Now she is a wife, mother, and graphic designer. But alongside all those titles that she dreamed of and hoped for, there was another one recently added to her résumé that she wasn't expecting: the role of caregiver for her mother.

When she was thirty-six weeks pregnant, Hannah received the most unexpected news. Her mother was rushed to the emergency room for brain surgery and was admitted to the neurology ICU. What was supposed to be a time of new life and celebration quickly turned into desperation, pivoting, and having to mother her mother alongside being a mother-to-be herself. It turned out that Hannah's mom had a subarachnoid hemorrhage, which is one of the deadliest strokes a person can have.[1] It was a genuine miracle that she survived and that they were able to get her through the surgery, but one of the long-lasting effects on Hannah's mother was a type of vascular dementia that still affects her to this day.

Suffering can certainly shake our beliefs, and this was the case for Hannah. Though she knew God was good and trustworthy, something as sudden and tragic as this did cause her to question His character and plans. I think any of us would have done the same.

Maybe you, too, have gone through a season where it felt like God did a 180 on your life and nothing was making sense. You reminded Him of what He did for others and questioned why He didn't do it for you: the healing, the miracle, the restoration. Doubt began to creep in, and you wondered whether God really is who He says He is. But here is where Hannah's story reveals the redemption of God in the changes she wasn't prepared for: She still went to God when it felt like a wrestle. She brought Him her honest questions, her real doubts, her anger, grief, and confusion—all of it. And in it all, she didn't lose hope or forsake her faith. Instead of pushing God away, she approached Him, embraced Him, and invited Him to do what only He could do with her and her mother's lives. She knew that her hard and heavy emotions could coexist with surrender and hope in God's redemptive plans.

Hannah told me that when she started to bring her grief, anger, sadness, and doubts to God, she began to experience His peace, comfort, and strength. When she welcomed Him into the pain, He began to work on her heart. He patiently waited for her to approach Him, even as she wrestled with questions of why and doubt, and continued to be patient with her as she honestly and openly unpacked every grievance that was burdening her.

Not only has Hannah been able to encounter the Lord's peace and provision in all this in the most unexpected ways, but she has been able to develop a refined faith in God, a deeper love for God, a greater trust in God, and a greater knowledge that even if things were to remain like this for her mother and her family forever, God is still good, still has good plans for her and her family, and will work this out for good. Hannah knew that doubt wasn't the opposite of faith in God, but that for the Christian, it is often part of the journey we are all on.

Don't Demonize Your Doubt

I know that for some of us, based on our specific upbringings, *doubt* is seen as a dirty word, a forbidden struggle, and a great sign of weakness. But doubt is a very normal obstacle we run into in our faith walk. Tim Keller wrote, "A faith without some doubts is like a human body without any antibodies in it."[2] I believe that if we were never faced with doubt, then there would be a lack of genuineness and depth to the convictions we hold. Author Paul Tillich wrote, "Doubt is not the opposite of faith; it is one element of faith."[3] For that very reason, I don't think it is fair for Christians to demonize our doubt. What if instead of shaming ourselves and others for the doubts we expressed because of our traumas, circumstances, and suffering, we saw it as a chance for our beliefs to be tested, strengthened, and grown? Doubt doesn't have to be the end of the journey; it can be a catalyst for real faith to take root and strongly hold us upright.

> Doubt doesn't have to be the end of the journey; it can be a catalyst for real faith to take root and strongly hold us upright.

Thomas was one of Jesus' disciples, and he was given the nickname "doubting Thomas" in the church. Listen, if I were Thomas, I think I might have a bone to pick with the grapevine of sermon titles because John got "the beloved disciple" and Peter got "the rock." As much as Thomas's testimony includes doubt, there is a huge turn of faith we see at the end of his story. If anything, I would think that through his story of redemption, we would call him "believing Thomas." Maybe that nickname can stick starting today!

So what is Thomas's story? Where did this nickname come from? After the crucifixion of Jesus, many of the disciples were discouraged that their beloved Savior and rabbi had been brutally killed in front of them. Friday evening passed, Saturday went by, and then came Sunday—resurrection Sunday, to be exact. Jesus rose from the dead! The women went to the tomb to finish taking care of His corpse, only to find Him risen from the grave. Mary Magdalene informed the disciples of this, but they were left in disbelief. Eventually, though, ten of the disciples were visited by the risen Christ Himself while congregating in the upper room. They were overjoyed at the sight of Him! Their hope was restored, their faith was reignited, and they were commissioned to be at peace by Christ Himself (John 20:19–22). But guess who was missing from the mix? Thomas.

Imagine all your friends being in the room where it happened, and you are left on the outskirts like Aaron Burr (shout-out to all my *Hamilton* fanatics out there). We read in John 20:24–29 about how, when Thomas returned, the disciples told him all about what had happened. His response was: "Unless I see the nail marks in his hands and put my finger where the nails were, and put my hand into his side, I will not believe" (v. 25). Some of us might read this story and roll our eyes at Thomas. Maybe you're even thinking to yourself, *Thomas, you idiot! You were literally walking alongside Jesus! You saw every miracle, heard every sermon, and followed Him faithfully all this time. Why on earth would you not believe?*

Others of us may immediately side with Thomas, thinking, *Yeah, Thomas. How come everyone else gets their miracle and sees Jesus move in extraordinary ways, and I'm always left out?* I don't blame you one bit if that's you today, because that's been me plenty of times throughout various seasons. I know some people have judged me for my doubts and my desire for concrete evidence from God, but it's not because I don't trust in Him; it's because, in my heart, I couldn't bear to get my hopes up again.

We can't forget that Thomas just lost one of his best friends. He was in deep grief. He was disappointed and downcast. The radical change from walking with Jesus earlier that week to seeing Him nailed to a cross, bloodied and beaten, is unbelievably hard for any human to process and make sense of. He wasn't rebelling in his doubt or discrediting his faith in God. Thomas was heartbroken and defeated. Let's give doubting Thomas some grace here because if I witnessed my friend getting tortured and murdered before my very eyes, and heard they were walking around a few days later in a glorified body, I would need some convincing too.

A whole week went by, and then suddenly, Jesus appeared to them again. This time, Thomas was in the room where it happened. The doors were locked, Jesus showed up out of nowhere, and He said to Thomas, "Put your finger here; see my hands. Reach out your hand and put it into my side. Stop doubting and believe" (John 20:27).

Jesus wasn't saying these things to shame Thomas. He wasn't trying to make Thomas look like a fool for struggling to believe after an earth-shattering event. Jesus, being the good God that He is, met Thomas with compassion. He showed up and proved Himself to be true amid Thomas's doubts. Jesus knew that Thomas needed this moment, even if it happened a week later. And Thomas went on to exclaim, "My Lord and my God!" (v. 28). This is the pinnacle moment of this story for Thomas: a confession and conviction that Jesus Christ is God in the flesh. This is the belief we Christians bet our lives on! This is the conclusion Thomas came to in his journey from doubt to declaration. Jesus Christ is Lord; He is the resurrection and the life!

Thomas's doubts didn't disqualify him. As we know from church tradition, he went on to preach the gospel to the region of India and was eventually martyred for his faith. He went from a doubter to a martyr. That encounter with the risen Christ launched him to an unapologetic and bold life of missions. Doubting Thomas, or should I say *believing* Thomas, had a radical transformation from unbelief to belief, and so can we!

Jesus wants to meet us in our doubt. He does so at the right time, in the right way, at the right place. Jesus also wants us to approach Him in our doubt and bring to Him the questions, the burdens, the unmet expectations, and the things we believed for that didn't come to pass. He will meet us as we carry those burdens, and He will take them from us, lightening our load so that we don't have to do life alone any longer. There will be a resolution, and there will be redemption, sometimes in the way we had hoped for and other times in ways we didn't expect.

From Disappointment to Divine Appointment

Another story I am reminded of, which displays the resurrection power of Jesus and how He is always on time—even when it feels delayed on our end—is the story of Lazarus in John 11:38–44. Lazarus, the brother of Martha and Mary, was sick, so they sent word to Jesus to come and heal their brother. Jesus showed up four days later, taking His time to get there, only to pull up to a grieving and mourning Martha, asking where He had been. Mary didn't come out to meet him because she was so overwhelmed with disappointment and doubt. But what felt like disappointment, delay, and fertile soil for doubt led to a divine appointment instead.

They got something better than healing; they got to see a dead man walking.

Jesus raised Lazarus from the dead after giving Martha a loving theological lesson on how He was and is the resurrection and the life (v. 25). I think some of us need to believe this today—that Jesus can resurrect, revive, restore, and redeem the things we have discredited as dead and gone. The dreams that have died, the hope that has died, and the faith that has died. Maybe the miracle of revival in your life isn't about a someone or a something but your faith in Jesus! After all, He is the founder and perfecter of it (Hebrews 12:2 ESV).

When we experience doubts, delays, disappointments, and even deaths of certain things in life, sometimes our faith and hope get dragged down with them. But I am here to tell you today that God is faithful, good, and still shows up. Jesus didn't judge or critique the two grieving women who were questioning why He didn't show up when their brother—whom Jesus loved—was sick and died; He wept with them (John 11:35). He got right there with them in the mess of it all. But He also had an end in mind that they didn't expect. Jesus had them roll away the gravestone, and as He called out for Lazarus, Jesus' resurrection power revived him.

Friend, this is the God we serve. The One who calls forth life out of death and hope out of heartbreak. I don't know what gravestones He might move in your story, but what I do know is that we can hope in Jesus' resurrection power to bring redemption and purpose to where there was once only hopelessness and doubt.

Space for Mystery and Wonder

Faith requires us to trust a known God with the unknown. It's in that space of mystery and surrender that we choose to believe in who God is, what He has said, and what He has done. I always tell people who ask about the Christian faith that even if we had 99 percent certainty, understanding, and knowledge, there would still be at least a 1 percent element of faith in our walk with God. There will always be an opportunity where God asks us to trust Him to do what only He can do. But this doesn't have to be a scary thing, nor does it have to be a place for doubt to drag us down. What if instead of this space of unknown breeding doubt in our walk, it bred wonder and awe for God? What if instead of the unknown separating us from God, it stitched us into closer intimacy with God?

The English bishop J. C. Ryle, in his work *Holiness*, talked about how even when we cannot see what is ahead, we should find contentment in clinging to our faith when we have no sight.[4] After all, this is the heart of 2 Corinthians 5:7. I hold on to this with hope, knowing that I do not walk blindly; I walk with a confident trust that God knows where we are going. I see Him clearly even when the path isn't. I can step into the unknown because I know my God, my Guide.

Sometimes the steps of faith He calls us to take make no sense in that moment, but as we look back on our lives months and years from now, it will be abundantly clear what God was up to. I know that faith isn't a cakewalk, and sometimes it feels like we are balancing on a tightrope with a blindfold over our eyes. Faith requires an element of risk, an element of the unknown. But that doesn't have to be a bad thing. In fact, I believe that living by faith is one of the most exciting adventures of our lives. Instead of anxiety, there is excitement to be had, knowing that we trust in the One who is in complete control.

Some of us today might be dwelling on the anxiety of the unknown a bit too heavily, and I get that. There have been seasons when the mysteries of "what if" and "what's next" caused me to spiral, to doubt, and to jump into action to try to orchestrate everything to go my way. That's partially because of the environment I grew up in; when something wasn't going according to plan, you fought and strived to correct its course. But when we choose to submit and commit our lives to following Jesus, we have to let go of the helm and allow the breath of God to steer our ships in the direction His winds take us.

You and I are called to trust, yield, and dwell in Christ—to move toward Him in the mystery because He gives us solid ground to stand on. He gives us a lamp that lights the next step of our path, not the entire road (Psalm 119:105). I think Philip Yancey encapsulated this well when he wrote: "Faith means trusting in advance what will only make sense in reverse."[5] There are steps that won't make sense and plot twists in the chapters of our lives that make us want to skip ahead to read the resolution, but doing life with Christ means meeting Him in the mysteries and trusting His timing and pace of working out all things for good in our lives (Romans 8:28).

Our finite minds cannot fully comprehend the will and ways of God. Doubt tries to serve us by filling in the unknown space with assumptions and explanations, but maybe it's best to let God speak into the space and remind us of His goodness and faithfulness. Deuteronomy 29:29 tells us that there are things that only God knows about, and He is accountable for those things. Rather than spending our time worrying, doubting, and catastrophically thinking about every possible scenario and outcome, what if we accepted that our God is sovereign over the unknown parts of our lives? What if we chose to believe the truth that He cares deeply about our stories—even more than we do? What if trusting God in the unknown wasn't just an act of faith but an act of wisdom and worship?

> Worship recognizes the majesty, power, authority, and nature of who God is, and a life lived in mystery, wonder, faith, and trust is just that.

Worship recognizes the majesty, power, authority, and nature of who God is, and a life lived in mystery, wonder, faith, and trust is just that. Where doubt once overstayed and occupied every corner of our lives, it is now time for it to be escorted out, making room for worship and wonder to come in, renovate, and redeem the story you're living with the Lord. Don't underestimate the importance of wonder in your walk as a believer! Wonder makes room for God to move miraculously. It is time to let faith arise like an anthem along with your banner of hope, declaring not just with words but with our lives: "Jesus, You are worthy and wonderful! I trust in You!"

He Won't Leave You to Drown

If you grew up attending Sunday school or are an avid fan of *The Chosen*, I'm sure you've heard or seen the story of Jesus and Peter walking on water. This takes place in Matthew 14:22–33. Jesus had just finished feeding thousands of people and decided to send His disciples ahead of Him to sail to their next destination while He withdrew in prayer with the Father.

Even Jesus needed that quality time to close the door behind Him and get into God's presence. If the Son of God did, how much more should we prioritize that?

While sailing across the Sea of Galilee, a great storm turned up out of nowhere, sending the disciples into a panic. The winds were pushing them all over the place. The waves were knocking them off-balance and off course. This didn't seem to be going according to plan.

Then, in the early morning hours of their tossing and turning—stomachs churning and hearts yearning for any sort of relief—they saw what looked like a ghost on the water. They shouted in fear and terror, only to realize it was Jesus walking on the water. Jesus showed up!

He shouted these reassuring words over the roaring waves, "Don't be afraid.... Take courage. I am here!" (14:27 NLT). Now, here is where it gets interesting, as if this wasn't already a sight to behold. Peter, in his audacious boldness, yelled out to Jesus, "Lord, if it's really you, tell me to come to you, walking on the water" (v. 28 NLT). And if you know how the story goes, then you know what Jesus said to him next: "Yes, come" (v. 29 NLT).

I would have been shaking in my sandals if I were Peter. Imagine crawling out of that boat onto the waters that were just trying to drown you. Peter made the brave move to literally get out of the boat and head out to Jesus the second He said to come to Him. How many of us pause to recognize that before Peter started to sink beneath the waves (spoiler alert), he dared to believe and got out of the boat? He dared to hope, stepping out of what everyone would claim is the safest place—the boat—and made His way toward Jesus, the safest person.

For a moment, Peter had his eyes locked on Jesus, and he began to walk on the water toward Him. I imagine that James and John wished they had made that call now that they were stuck watching from the sidelines. Sons of thunder? More like signs and wonders! I bet they couldn't believe their eyes with what they were beholding! In fact, Peter began to doubt what his eyes were seeing. He took his

The Fabric of Hope

eyes off Jesus, focusing on the winds and waves that were roaring and rushing instead, and became fearful. Immediately, he began to sink before his Savior.

I don't know if you've ever had a near-death experience with drowning, but I have. When I was eight years old, my dad came down to visit my brother and me during the summer, and he took us to a well-known water park outside of San Antonio, Texas, called Schlitterbahn. I decided to go to the wave pool where hundreds of people were wading in their floaties, getting thrown around by the monstrous waves. I was swimming around, trying to find an open floatie, when suddenly water crashed over me and sent me tumbling under the surface. That's when I got caught underneath the inner tube of a larger adult. I couldn't get out from underneath as she moved in toward her friends. I was stuck, hitting the tube as hard as I could to get her attention, but slowly I began to grow weak and tired. My vision started to fade. Things were beginning to turn black.

I kicked my legs with one last attempt right into that person's side. Immediately, she pulled me out from underneath her and the water, and I started gasping for air. Now, here's the thing: I was expecting her to check my vitals to see if I was okay, but instead, she and her friends yelled at me and tossed me to the side. I guess it was rude of me to fight for my life and flail while suffocating and inching closer to meeting my Maker. I remember exactly how I felt in that moment: afraid, hopeless, abandoned, and out of options. I can only imagine it was ten times scarier for Peter to be drowning in the middle of a storm on a sea.

Peter cried out to Jesus to save him as he was sinking, and Jesus, unlike the person in the wave pool, did just that. He immediately grabbed Peter's arm and pulled him up. Peter, the fisher of men, did not end up sleeping with the fishes. Once Peter got into the saving grasp of Jesus, head above the waters, Jesus said to him, "You of little faith . . . why did you doubt?" (v. 31). Yes, this was a moment of rebuke toward Peter. Yes, Peter had every reason to trust Jesus and have faith that he would be okay. But even in this rebuke that redirected Peter to remember who Jesus was and all that He was capable of as his Lord and Savior, Jesus did not let Peter sink.

Some of us today are ashamed that we have doubted God in certain areas of our struggles, and we have believed the lie that because we have questioned or doubted God, He will leave us to drown just to prove a point. Friend, that is not the heart of God. That is a lie from the pit of hell. Jesus is a Savior. He came to this world to die the death you and I deserved and rose three days later because He wanted to save us. He went into the depths so that we wouldn't drown, so that we could have real, full lives in Him and with Him (John 10:10).

He had grace for us then and has grace for us now in the difficulties, doubts, and drowning. He knows that our uncertainties and reservations are real and that they stem from how we were let down by others or traumatized by the world. However, He invites us to call out to Him and be lifted out of skepticism into safety, security, and submission to Him. Jesus reached for Peter in his doubt; He did not reject him. Neither will He reject you. He will reach for you.

Bring Him Your Questions, Comments, and Concerns

It is okay to wrestle with doubt, but like my bestie Hannah, we must bring our questions, comments, and concerns to the Lord. He will clear His name even if He doesn't clear up the chaos in the way we expect, demand, or desire. Sometimes He does clear it up and removes the waves that keep whacking us, but other times He calls us to walk on those waves to meet Him. To be near our Savior in the middle of the storm.

Time and time again, He meets us where we are. He reaches out to us and doesn't reject us. He strengthens our faith and shows Himself to be kind and trustworthy. Faithful and worthy of our faith. This was the ultimate conclusion Hannah arrived at. And she fully believes this! Even though she never asked for this storm to pass over her, she knows God can still redeem this situation and use it for greater glory. Rainbows come after the rain, and she is starting to see the wonder and colors of joy surface once again in her life.

Truth be told, this story of hers is still being written and woven together. Even though there has been progress, her mother is still not fully restored to her pre-incident self. Would you join me in lifting up Hannah and her mother in prayer as you read this? Although she now has systems in place that provide her mother with support, she is still processing this change, moving from doubt to trust, from wondering why to embracing God's wonder and will.

I know we want all the information about what seasons we will encounter or how to navigate the storm we are in today, but maybe we need to have the courage to say yes to God in the mystery—to declare that we still believe in the Bible's unchanging truths when the seasons of life change and storms roll in. I know a thing or two about this kind of unpredictability as a Texan, trust me! It'll be sunny one minute, tornadoes the next, and then a hailstorm will blow through. That's just a normal Tuesday in DFW! Yet, I have still chosen to root my life in this crazy-weather state I so love because my love for it far outweighs the storms I know will come. I know that we can weather the storms that literally come because my home's foundation is firm here. Likewise, I know that whatever storms life throws my way won't knock me down either because my foundation of hope is firm in Jesus.

I know we all want to read the stories of how God did the miracle, did the full restoration, did the exceedingly and abundantly more blessing as He did with Peter and Thomas, but sometimes the miracle looks a little different. Sometimes we have a story like Hannah's, where we are still in the middle of what God is writing.

God's will doesn't always go our way, and that can lead us to doubt and reconsider whether we believe in who God says He is. But doubt can lead to a deepened faith if we acknowledge it before the Lord, reexamine it through the lens of truth, and allow Him to prove His goodness in saving us and showing up. Who's to say there isn't a miracle in the making on the other side of the waiting?

The Fabric of Hope

How we respond to what God wills or allows matters a great deal. When things don't go as we planned, hoped, expected, or prayed for, we can respond in one of two ways: rejection and animosity or redirection and acceptance. As much as doubt can be one of our greatest roadblocks, I also believe it is one of the best obstacles we can overcome. Doubt gives us the unique opportunity to either question God and run away or have wonder and draw closer to God, knowing and believing that we will get a front-row seat to watch His redemptive hand at work. This is what we can hope for. Jesus is who we can hope in.

Chapter 8

LET HOPE ANCHOR YOUR HEART

There are no coincidences in the life of a Christian, just God's divine and detailed involvement and intervention. I've had friends call those moments "Godwinks,"[1] and my mom would even say those times were "God-incidences." One specific Godwink I am reminded of happened just before my mom passed away. Now, I am not saying that my mom's death was God nudging me with a wink. The moment I am specifically thinking of was the morning before she died. I remember going to my apartment complex's pool, and it was just me, my Bible, and God. For three days I had been praying to God, weeping before Him, seeking His answers, and pleading for His intervention to renew my mom's life and restore her to full health. But oddly enough, and by *oddly* I mean *godly*, whenever I would turn my face to God and lay my requests before Him, He would fill me with a certain kind of peace that suggested He would be bringing her home and that I could grieve with hope. Yes, I still prayed for a miracle and believed with my whole heart that God could certainly bring her out of this, but He kept assuring me throughout the entire process that He was bringing her home—a different but full and complete healing.

As much as it was gut-wrenching to accept that my mother was no longer going to be with me on this side of heaven, I was full of the peace of God through it all. I specifically remember Him speaking so clearly to me after I read Psalm 121 the morning of her passing, *Kirby, you get to grieve with hope.* This was such a significant statement of truth and comfort God gave me, especially because I have also grieved without hope.

Not only did I lose my mother, who struggled with alcoholism, but I also lost my father at an early age to his own battle with alcoholism. I was only ten years old, and this was four years before I gave my life to Christ. Although I had been reassured by family members and loved ones that *Dad was in a better place*, I felt like I had no hope in my grief. The change was overwhelming, the emptiness felt so heavy, and the pain was soul-crushing. It was a lot for a ten-year-old to process. But when my mom died when I was twenty-six, there was something that made the grieving process different:

my hope in Jesus Christ as my Lord and Savior. Not only that, but I knew my mom had professed her faith in Christ as her Lord and Savior too. He was her hope as well.

I bring this up because a good friend of mine, Michael, reached out to me during all this to check in on me as I grieved. He was a consistent source of prayer and encouragement for me in that season, and as I approached the one-year anniversary of my mom's passing, the grief started to hit me not in waves but tsunamis. Coincidentally—I mean *God-incidentally*—his mentor, Steve Carter, was about to release a book right around the time of that anniversary. Michael sent me a copy of it, and when I read it, I felt like God winked at me from heaven. Steve Carter, author and speaker, wrote in his book, *Grieve, Breathe, Receive*, about how, during his own grief journey, what made it different for him was that he was able to grieve with hope because of the hope found in Christ.[2]

Grieve with hope.

I couldn't believe I was reading those words. Those were the same words God spoke to me just a year earlier! Those were the same words I death-gripped as I navigated the death of my mother. This was certainly a Godwink.

Fast-forward a few months, I was sitting in the back row of the church auditorium with my arms crossed instead of in the front row with my hands lifted high, wondering whether I could trust this speaker to share anything that would minister to the pain I was feeling. Truth be told, the entire congregation was going through its own season of grief after a sin our pastor had kept secret had been exposed. We all felt betrayed by this man who was supposed to be living an honest, righteous life of integrity. The grief ran deep and wide within us all.

This guest speaker walked onto the stage, and like many of the other attendees, I was skeptical, afraid to trust any leaders to speak into my life in this season of shock. But this speaker gave us a message of hope that not only began healing the hurt in my heart that had been burdening me in this long and painful season, but he delivered a whole sermon on how we can dare to hope and grieve with hope in any season of loss or disappointment.

Grieve with hope? There was that phrase again! Another Godwink in a season of so much grief.

It wasn't until about halfway through the sermon that I realized the guest speaker was none other than Steve Carter, the author of the book that I read when my mom died. I don't even know if I would call it a Godwink at that point because it was like a holy slap in the face—in the best way. We were all moved to tears by this truthful, timely message, and once I had collected myself after his sermon was finished, I messaged him on Instagram. As it turned out, Steve had been following me ever since my mom died because of what Michael shared with him about my grief journey, and he was keeping up with all my posts online. One thing led to another, and he ended up guesting on my podcast not even a few weeks later to talk about this idea of grieving with hope.[3]

During our interview, he mentioned how we have such a skewed view of what hope is. So many of us wake up and *hope* that the rain will stop before we have to run out to our car, or *hope* that we get that extra scoop of chicken in our Chipotle order without having to pay extra for it, or *hope* we get the callback for the audition we've been preparing for, or *hope* that our spouse will get the promotion after years of working at the company. That kind of hope is centered around *uncertainty*. It's a maybe. It's a cross-my-fingers kind of yearning. But is that really hope, the hope that's described in Scripture?

Biblical hope rests on assurance and full confidence. It's not just "*God willing*, this thing will happen," but instead, "God *wills* this thing to happen." The things He calls us to hope in are concrete, God-willed, and faithfully forged!

We can have sure hope in many things! How He wills for us to be saved and in relationship with Him (1 Timothy 2:4), to be comforted in our pain (2 Corinthians 1:3–4), to be sanctified and renewed (Titus 3:5), and to see His goodness flow forth in our lives (Psalm 27:13). We have hope in the first foundational fact that God is exactly who He says He is. This gives us the confidence to have faith in the unseen and what is to come.

You see, biblical hope is rooted in promise. Hebrews 6:17–20 states that we, as believers, have hope as an anchor for our souls, hope in salvation and eternal life: that God will redeem and bless His people, and that Jesus, as our High Priest, goes before us to advocate and reconcile us back to God. We can put our full weight on these promises and believe they will hold

> Hope is confident assurance and trust in what is true and proven—God's personhood, promises, patterns, and presence!

us up. Why? Because this hope is confident assurance and trust in what is true and proven—God's personhood, promises, patterns, and presence!

Biblical hope does not falter or fail, because it is anchored in the truth, not our feelings. When life hits us from every side and we feel fragile spiritually and emotionally, God's unchanging character and promises remain steadfast and true. He was the One I clung to when I needed the will to keep moving forward.

You can keep clinging to the hope of who God is when the leaders in your life show their true colors; God is unchanging (Hebrews 13:8).

You can keep clinging to the hope of what God can do with the mustard-seed-sized faith you have in the deliverance of your prodigal child; God is faithful (2 Timothy 2:13).

You can keep clinging to the hope of how God can rewrite the endings of our stories we thought we had forever messed up due to our faithlessness and relapsing; God is a redeemer (Joel 2:25).

When everything else doesn't go according to plan, we reorient ourselves to hope in God and His perfect plans. After all, He is the God who brings life to where there was once loss (Isaiah 61:3), confidence where there was once confusion (Proverbs 3:5–6), and peace where there was once panic (1 Corinthians 14:33).

God Can Hold Up Our Hope

When I was a competitive cheerleader, I was always the base. That meant that I was at the bottom of the pyramid, holding the girls up, throwing them in the air, and catching them as they came down. Those girls put their full weight on me, confidently trusting that they could stand on me because I had the ability, strength, and consistency to hold them up. Time and time again in practice, this was proven to be true. Whenever competition day came, they knew they were not going to fall . . . okay, maybe sometimes they did, but look—I am not a perfect person. But Jesus is (Hebrews 4:15)! The most confident and consistent supporter (2 Thessalonians 3:3), He will hold you up securely and safely (Psalm 18:2). He is the steady base, the firm foundation, that we can put our full weight on (1 Corinthians 3:11). We can stand firm because He is faithful to fulfill every promise (2 Timothy 2:13); what He promises will be done (Numbers 23:19), and everything He wills will happen (Isaiah 46:9–10). You and I can have confident hope that He is faithful in all He does and will always be true to His character (Lamentations 3:22–23). We can dare to hope, grieve with hope, and rest in hope, knowing that our hope is secure. We can stand firm on the steady base that is Christ!

What if we dared to have that kind of hope and shifted our hearts and minds to have a reason to hope when changes happen, when storms arise, when grief hits, and when the unlikely and undesirable become a foreseeable future? We can have hope. Biblical hope. Confident hope.

Hope reminded me and assured me that my God goes before me (Deuteronomy 31:8), that He would see me through to the other side (Isaiah 43:2), that nothing would be wasted in the season I was in (Romans 8:28), and that it would be used for the glory of God

(1 Corinthians 10:31), the development of my character and spiritual maturity (James 1:2–4), and for the good of those witnessing me live a life following after Christ (Matthew 5:16).

Now maybe you're thinking to yourself, *Okay, God. I think I've gone through enough refining. I think I am spiritually mature enough now. Can we be done?* I get it. I have pleaded that petition to the Lord too. I have felt tired, worn out, and wondered if the refining and enduring would ever end, not just in the past but even recently with my chronic migraines and all the ailments that follow. But friend, just because the flames of the refining fire are still burning doesn't mean that God has forgotten or forsaken you. Neither does it mean He is ignoring your prayers and pleas.

I know how hard the growing pains can be. I am, of course, speaking spiritually, because I stopped growing after eighth grade. I am five foot three and proud! I have earned some spiritual stretch marks over the years of growing, thanks to certain seasons of life. In the maturing, growing, and forming, I have learned that God isn't being cruel when we go through growth; it is a sign of His kindness that He walks alongside us from infancy to maturity in Him.

As He renews us daily, He remains with us. Second Corinthians 4:16–18 is proof of this, saying, "Therefore we do not lose heart. Though outwardly we are wasting away, yet inwardly we are being renewed day by day. For our light and momentary troubles are achieving for us an eternal glory that far outweighs them all. So we fix our eyes not on what is seen, but on what is unseen, since what is seen is temporary, but what is unseen is eternal." When the going got tough and the enduring felt like an eternity, I knew I could always call upon Christ to renew me every single day with the strength, patience, hope, joy, discipline, faith, and everything else I needed to survive and thrive in every season of life. This is our hope for this side of heaven!

He also reminded me that He wants to share the weight of what feels like a burden to me (Matthew 11:28–30). These things that once burdened me do not outweigh the weight of glory that is to come! What is that glory that is to come, exactly? Freedom and joy in Christ (Romans 8:18–21), God's presence in which sorrow and suffering and sin are no more (Revelation 21:3–4), glorified and whole bodies in which our pain and diseases will no longer afflict us (1 Corinthians 15:42–44), and eternity with our risen Savior (John 17:3).

Along with that, God repositioned me so that I could see things from His point of view: *eternity*. I don't know if you reflect on your life and it feels like it all went by in the blink of an eye, but it feels that way for me. My childhood in New Jersey, the highs and lows of middle school, the days I spent attending summer camp, the hours of rehearsals for my high school theater productions, the weeks of studying to earn my degree while battling chronic migraines, the months of writing my books and sermons, and even the years I spent with my mom when she was alive. It has all been a blip in the timeline and tapestry of my life. Presently, the afflictions I go through feel like forever. But every time I've crossed the finish line, stepped into the light, and made it to the other side, I reflect that it actually went by quite quickly.

As I've pressed into the Lord and prayed for healing and resolve, I have also prayed for repositioning in my point of view, not that I would just escape the season I am in but that I would be able to look at it with eternity in mind right now. All this is temporary, yet it serves a necessary purpose, and it could be one that I may or may not understand right now. What I do know is that His renewing and repositioning of my outlook on endurance has given me the motivation, discipline, and faith to keep moving forward, knowing it will all mean something and grow into something purposeful. The growing pains bring about maturity, completion, and intimacy with God that otherwise wouldn't be possible, and I wouldn't trade them for anything!

Is This Verse Actually About Us?

Hope is not throwing our wishes into the wind and seeing where they land. Neither is it a roll of the dice or a game of Russian roulette. The hope Christians have is firmly fixed on the promises of God. He cannot go against His Word. We can confidently cling to His vows, oaths, promises, and covenants. But we need to approach His Word and promises with context, not placing unrealistic expectations on God through eisegesis (reading the Word looking for *us* in every story) instead of exegesis (reading the Word contextually to understand what it meant *then* and *there*). Some promises in the Bible were made to specific people, during specific times, for specific reasons. Some examples include:

- The Promised Land (Genesis 12:7; Joshua 1:2–4): This promise was specifically made to Abraham and his descendants, the Israelite people. Genesis 15:18 clearly lays out the boundaries of this real plot of land from the Nile to the Euphrates. Some pastors take this to mean everything is "our promised land," and that we can walk into any "territory" of life, such as career goals and personal dreams, claiming it for ourselves in the name of God—but that isn't the proper application.
- The Blessings for Obedience (Deuteronomy 28:1–14): God made a covenant between Himself and the nation of Israel under the law of Moses, and if they were conditionally obedient to these laws, God promised them prosperity and victory in their lives and land. I've heard prosperity gospel preachers use this passage out of context to support the idea that God wants wealth and health for every Christian, and if you do "good things," then God will give you "good things," but that is a total misinterpretation and misapplication.

So what promises *do* apply to us? I'm glad you asked!

- We can have salvation in Christ by grace, through faith (Ephesians 2:8–9).
- We have access to the presence of God everywhere we go (Matthew 28:20).
- We cannot be separated from God's love (Romans 8:38–39).

- We have victory over sin and death because Christ won the victory over sin and death through the cross and His resurrection (1 Corinthians 15:57).
- We can have peace that surpasses all understanding through the power and presence of being in Christ (Philippians 4:6–7).
- We have the power of the Holy Spirit within us to fulfill what God has called us to do (Acts 1:8).
- We know that all things will be worked out for good for those who love God (Romans 8:28).
- We have hope for eternal life in Christ through the profession and confession of our faith in Him (Titus 1:2).

These are just a few of the promises I can list off the top of my head that were true for believers then but are also true for those of us centuries later. That is what hermeneutics teaches us. I hope you enjoyed this brief theology lesson today. I know it's a lot of big church words, but knowing these words, definitions, and how they apply to Scripture informs our lives, our relationship with God, and how we do ministry with others.

Now that we understand a bit more about the context of what we hope for in Scripture, I want to ask you a very important question: What do you need to hope for today?

Maybe you need to hope in the person of God—His kindness, goodness, and purpose in a season that seems meaningless.

Maybe you need to hope in the power of God—His justice,

vengeance, and great love for you as you face spiritual warfare from the world and the Enemy.

Maybe you need to hope in the promises of God—His redemptive work and ability to make all things new, such as your reputation and character, or the changes and losses you've experienced, trusting that He will follow through on His vows to you.

Maybe you need to hope in God's plans—His perfect and pleasing will, in which nothing is wasted and all can be repurposed for greater glory in your story.

I know for some of us, hope has made us feel led on and strung out. But maybe it's because we were hoping in things that were outside of God and His will. When we can know contextually who it is we hope in and which promises are ours to cling to with confidence, we avoid the hurt we read about in Proverbs 13:12: "Hope delayed makes the heart sick, but desire fulfilled is a tree of life" (CSB). We don't have to feel deferred and defeated by unmet expectations any longer. Biblical hope, contextual hope, and hermeneutic hope give us something to ground ourselves in so that we can wait with confidence for what will arrive, be restored, or be renewed in God's perfect timing.

Living with Lasting Hope

If I were to ask you, "Where does your help come from?" you may think of that one verse in Psalm 121 that declares how our help comes from the Lord. But I have an additional question I want to ask you today: Where does your *hope* come from?

For me, it has been the Lord. When I try to place my hope in the ever-changing things of this world, the created things, the broken things, and the finite things, I end up building on a foundation that is like sinking sand. It can't bear the weight and fully support the concrete things I am hoping for. Jesus spoke to this sentiment in Matthew 7:24–27. He said:

> "Therefore everyone who hears these words of mine and puts them into practice is like a wise man who built his house on the rock. The rain came down, the streams rose, and the winds blew and beat against that house; yet it did not fall, because it had its foundation on the rock. But everyone who hears these words of mine and does not put them into practice is like a foolish man who built his house on sand. The rain came down, the streams rose, and the winds blew and beat against that house, and it fell with a great crash."

The words of Jesus are a firm foundation we can build our lives upon, friend! The Bible is the inspired and inerrant Word of God. When we recognize Christ as our Lord and His Word as true, we can place our hope in Him and begin to build on it as a firm and secure foundation. We can take the promises, commands, and words of wisdom given throughout Scripture and apply them to our lives, building upon them like bricks, knowing that we will have a sturdy and steady house that can withstand anything that tries to come against it.

Jesus said in this specific teaching that the rain *will* come, the streams *will* rise, and the winds *will* pick up. That adds up, because if you've checked the news lately, I know you know that we live in a broken world, influenced by the decisions of broken people; sometimes those troubles are even a result of our own faulty decisions. Hardship and suffering *will* inevitably happen. Unpleasant and uninvited troubles *will* eventually come knocking, but that doesn't mean you have to get knocked down or stay knocked down.

Our metaphorical house doesn't have to succumb to the changing seasons and storms, because when we have a firm and fixed foundation, we can have confident hope that we *will* make it through. We *will* endure. We *will* last.

First Samuel 2:2 says, "There is none holy like the LORD: for there is none besides you; there is no rock like our God" (ESV). No other foundation can hold us up and support us like Jesus can. Not money, not accomplishments, not people-pleasing, not even our own strength can keep us steady. There is no rock like the Rock!

Psalm 18:2 says, "The LORD is my rock and my fortress and my deliverer, my God, my rock, in whom I take refuge, my shield, and the horn of my salvation, my stronghold" (ESV). We can run to God for refuge, protection, covering, and safety. He alone saves and is immovable whenever winds try to shake us and break us.

> We can have confident hope that we *will* make it through. We *will* endure. We *will* last.

Some of us run to toxic relationships, thinking we will find security and protection there, and others of us flee to accolades, thinking they will be enough. But only Christ is enough: big enough, strong enough, secure enough, and reliable enough to remain when the waters rush over us and take everything else with them. Your hope can endure, and your life will be secure in every storm when the Rock is your foundation, when He is the One in whom you anchor your hope (Hebrews 6:19–20). Rely on Him. Hope in Him. Put your weight on Him. He can carry your burdens, sustain you in your weakness, refresh your weary soul, and hold you up when you need that extra push to keep moving forward.

Know that hope is something we hold on to that comes with an added blessing: not just the coming promises and redemption of God but also the development of godly character. Romans 5:3–5 says, "Not only so, but we also glory in our sufferings, because we know that suffering produces perseverance; perseverance, character; and character, hope. And hope does not put us to shame, because God's love has been poured out into our hearts through the Holy Spirit, who has been given to us." The Holy Spirit has been given to us out of God's love, and He gives us the power to push forward and dare to hope.

So, friend, will you dare with me? Believing this season won't be wasted? Convinced God will do something greater through this than you could ever imagine? Assured that this will build your character and confidence in the risen Christ and the reality of His loving-kindness? Knowing that this will be used for greater glory in your life and the lives of those who are the lost, the least, the last, and the overlooked who need this hope themselves?

Your hope isn't a crutch, and your hope isn't wasted. Placed in Christ alone, your hope and life will be held by the same faithful, nail-marked hands that haven't let me go. Build your life upon Him, friend, and He won't let you go either.

Chapter 9

PEACE IN THE PIECES

Fun fact about me: When I gave my life to Christ at age fourteen, I thought my calling in life was to become a Christian rapper. Go on, get your laughs out. The funniest part was that I was so serious about this dream. I would come home from school, read my Bible, find some scripture that I liked, write raps, record them, and post them online so my friends could learn about Jesus. Don't worry; I scrubbed them from the internet once my frontal lobe developed. You don't need the image of me with a hat turned sideways, trying to be the female Christian Eminem. As ridiculous as it sounds—and was—it was actually a very sweet time between the Lord and me. I genuinely desired to see my friends understand Scripture and follow Christ, and I thought this was a creative and relevant way for them to learn it. The heart was there, but the talent, not so much.

Though I am not a Christian musician, over the years, I've become good friends with quite a few. One friend of mine is a Christian rapper named Hulvey. He has made some of my favorite Christian rap, specifically a song called "Holes."[1] The song focuses on how the holes in Christ's hands were the very things that brought healing to the holes in Hulvey's heart, a sentiment many Christians share. My favorite line in that song talks about how Jesus calmed the winds and the waves, and if He can do that, then there is no doubt He can calm the pain, fear, and hopelessness that we face. Cue it up and listen for those lyrics!

> If Jesus has the power to overcome the grave, we can also hope that He can restore life to us where we thought the Enemy had the final say.

I think they are brilliant because they are so true. Jesus Christ, our living hope, who conquered the grave, and who holds all authority, being God Himself, is not only the One who went to the cross, died, and rose again but is also the same One who was in the boat with His beloved disciples and calmed the winds and waves when they were afraid of the storm. If Jesus can calm the raging seas, we can also hope that He can calm the swirling storms that rock our boats. If Jesus has the power to overcome the grave, we can also hope that He can restore life to us where we thought the Enemy had the final say.

Jesus has all authority and all ability to act in accordance with His character, power, and will! Part of that character is loving us. Part of that power is being Lord of all. Part of that will is staying by our side in every circumstance we face as believers. I especially love this song because Hulvey's lyrics specifically display how all creation must obey and come to peace under Christ. He orders the seas to be still. He commands the storm to calm. Order, peace, and calm: Those are the results of Christ's lordship over our storms. He does this with our anxious thoughts, troubled hearts, shaken bones, and weary souls, bringing us back to hope and assurance in Him.

Stillness When It Swells

The peace of God is unlike anything else. It truly surpasses all things because the peace of God brings a calmness to life's calamities that doesn't otherwise make sense. That's because it's otherworldly. Galatians 5:22–23 explains that peace is a fruit of the Holy Spirit abiding in us, and we in Him. The word used for peace is εἰρήνη in the Greek, transliterated as *eirēnē*, which means peace, harmony, or tranquility.[2] It stems from the Hebrew word for peace: *shalom*. *Shalom* does mean "peace" and is often used as a greeting among Jewish people, but the word is used throughout the Bible to specifically mean completeness, wholeness, safety, satisfaction, and blessing.[3] I especially love that idea of wholeness. Knowing Him and being in relationship with Him makes us whole. The Holy Spirit calls all things to come into order under God, to be made complete and whole, pieced together by peace.

I know that home was not a peaceful place for me as a child when my dad was relapsing and raging; the same was true for my household in high school when my mother was binge drinking most days. Everything felt out of order—disrupted, chaotic, and confusing. The floor was not lava, friend—it was eggshells. My nervous system was in a constant state of survival mode, and peace was hard to come by. However, whenever I would shut the door and sit at the feet of Jesus, weeping, praying, petitioning, and warring for the healing and deliverance of my mother, I was always overcome by God's perfect peace.

Peace in knowing that God was my keeper and my mother's.

Peace in knowing that God was in control when everything felt out of control.

Peace in knowing that God would protect me and give me wisdom to navigate this uneasy situation.

Peace in knowing that God was a perfect and present Father to me, who loved me and would guide me.

Peace in knowing that God is the Savior in this story, and that I didn't have to put all the pressure on myself to be the rescuer when I also need rescuing.

Jesus wants to bring peace to the chaos of your life today too. Peace to the high school students who didn't get into their dream school and feel like their life is over. Peace to the young woman who just went through a gut-wrenching heartbreak, who feels like her prayers have gone completely unanswered, and who is wondering whether there are any good men out there. Peace to the mother who is overwhelmed by the constant fighting with her spouse and is hanging on to a thread of hope for their prodigal child.

I know we've all lived different lives and walked in different shoes. Some people have comfortable gel-base sneakers, while others of us have had to run marathons in stilettos. It's painful. Maybe you've rolled a couple of ankles. You've tripped up and hurt yourself, while others have seamlessly jumped the hurdles. Some of us have experienced different chaos than others. Maybe instead of an addict as a parent, you had your worst critic lording over you. Maybe instead of having to be the one to hold everything together, you never could, and because of that, you always felt pressured to toss your emotions to the side, but now you're at your breaking point.

I just want you to know today that Jesus, the God of perfect order, is not intimidated by the chaos in your life. He is actually the only One who can piece together the shards that are sticking out and puncturing your lungs. He wants you to be able to breathe. To be at peace. The coolest part about Jesus' presence and peace is that even if the surrounding circumstances don't let up, when He is let in, things change. Our minds calm down from the spiraling, our heartbeats sync into a restful rhythm, and the worries we once lost ourselves in are suddenly in the hands of the One who can deal with them. He is perfect; therefore, His peace is perfect. Let the perfect God of perfect peace have His way in your world, bringing wholeness to what was once keeping you up at night. Peace might not eliminate the existence of every problem, but that's okay because peace is the presence of the person of Jesus; He is everywhere, all the time, pursuing us in and out of the chaos!

A TikTok Love Story

I never would have imagined that my love story would be a living picture of peace existing within chaos. I also never would have thought it would include TikTok, a Canadian, and a pandemic... but here I am—happily married since 2020 to my incredible husband, Richard. Okay, here's the backstory.

I have been creating comedic Christian content since 2012. That's where I got my start in creative evangelism online. As TikTok was becoming more popular, I decided to upload a silly little video with a Christian pickup line. Truth be told, I wasn't looking for a relationship or trying to win any hearts with this video. I genuinely thought it was funny and decided to upload it. In the video, I say, "You know what Scripture says: 'He who finds a wife finds a good thing.' How's it going? I'm good thing!" Funny pickup line, right?

I hit upload, went back to whatever I was doing, and about twenty minutes later decided to check on the video's progress. That's when I saw the funniest and smoothest response in my comment section. It read, "Hi, good thing, I'm he!" Get it? Because *he* who finds a wife finds a *good thing*? I was absolutely shaken by this because once I clicked on this random commenter's profile, my eyes were graced by the goodness of God's creation. This was the most attractive man I had ever seen in my life!

Peace in the Pieces

Listen, when I uploaded that video, I looked busted. I was in dirty sweatpants, hair undone, and barefaced; and that was this guy's first impression of me! I guess TikTok's For You Page really did its thing for Richard, because I really was for him (see what I did there?). I know we serve a perfect God because He knew exactly what He was doing having my video pop up on his phone.

The comment section quickly turned to DMs, which turned to texting, which turned to FaceTime calls, which ended up with me traveling up to Canada a month later in late January 2020. Deep down in my spirit, I knew that he was "the one." Side note, I always thought when people said, "When you know, you know," that it was the stupidest advice, but man, they were right! When you know, you know! And as I got to know Richard more, I knew that he was the one I wanted to spend the rest of my life with.

After months of long distance, traveling back and forth, and spending hours on the phone together, we finally made things official on my birthday, March 5, 2020. What we didn't expect, though, was that the world and its borders were about to shut down, marking the start of the global pandemic. Yep, I am talking COVID. On March 17, just a few weeks after we became official and professed our love to each other, the whole world shut down. As you likely know, it was a time full of so much chaos, disorder, loss, depression, unrest, contention, and isolation. Every single one of my speaking gigs and work opportunities was canceled, which meant I had no income for the foreseeable future. Every event was banned when social distancing was enacted, so all of my community was cut off. I was quarantined in my apartment completely alone for months, and nearly every city and country was on lockdown, which meant I could no longer visit Richard.

But in the middle of all this, I was also falling in love for the first time, experiencing all sorts of joy in this newfound relationship with the man I knew I wanted to spend the rest of my life with. I felt like a princess in her tower. Luckily, I had my Prince Charming, who I could talk to as the days and weeks passed. During that time, I got to know Richard, his heart for the Lord, and his desires and plans for the future—our future—even more. Eventually, as border restrictions began to lift, he was able to travel to the US. I couldn't have been more thankful to God. Finally, I could see him again, hug him again, and kiss him—mask to mask—again (surely you believe me on that, right?).

Now, I do want to step back from my little bubble of puppy love real quick and say that I know this was a period of time that affected everyone in the world very differently, very chaotically, and very intensely. I had family members and friends from all over the nation and world who were personally affected by COVID, and part of me felt guilty for having this pocket of peace in the middle of such a difficult and heartbreaking time for so many people. I had to walk six feet away from my friends through the loss of their loved ones, through the frustrations of civil unrest, and the discontentment of a world that had become so divided. From injections to injustice, everyone was going through something and either had an opinion on it or an objection to it. To try and put it simply, it was a rough time.

But as I've spent more time with God reflecting on this, I've realized that I approach many areas of my life with this sentiment: When times of grief happen, it's easy to feel guilty about embracing the beautiful, the wonderful, the joyful, and the peaceful parts that coexist alongside that. But I want to speak to that specifically, if that is you today.

In the middle of the storm, in the middle of the pain, in the middle of the chaos, God graces us with His peace, with beautiful blessings, and with pockets of hope and joy to cling to that give us life. I don't think we should feel guilty about embracing both the hope and the hard, the painful and the peaceful, the beauty and the broken. If anything, I think those are moments where God is showing us just how kind, loving, and good He still is. Even in the fragmented parts of life and fallen parts of our broken world, God, with His silver lining, can weave glimmers of grace in our story that carry us through with hope.

Richard was a glimmer of hope I got to cling to in a time when I otherwise would have been so alone, afraid, and angry with what was going on in the world. He was a grace and gift from God, and I don't take it for granted one bit. I'm sure if you were to look in your own life, you would see glimmers of God's grace shining with silver throughout the darkest parts of your story, gleaming like the stars in the night sky.

> Even in the fragmented parts of life and fallen parts of our broken world, God, with His silver lining, can weave glimmers of grace in our story that carry us through with hope.

I don't want you to dismiss the pockets of peace that He may be gifting you with in this season of hardship. Whether you feel guilty for embracing beauty when brokenness is still apparent, or whether you feel undeserving of the blessings God is giving you in your pain, I need you to know that God really is so kind that He gives us peace as a promise, not as a prize. That kind of peace can come in many forms: through people and community, through a slowed-down schedule and rest, through reading His Word and going to a worship night at your church, and even through food and laughter. You may be surprised to look around and see the glimmers of His grace and pieces of His peace sprinkled throughout your story being written today. Those moments and miracles are worth celebrating and praising Him for!

Receive that as an answer to prayer, a beacon of hope, and a gift from God that He is there with you, that He sees you, and that He is weaving good together even where there may be bad. That He is stitching in grace where there may be burdens. That He is mending in peace where there may be chaos. That He is ushering in new life where there once was death.

Peace Is Your Portion

I love what the prophet Isaiah wrote, "'Though the mountains be shaken and the hills be removed, yet my unfailing love for you will not be shaken nor my covenant of peace be removed,' says the LORD, who has compassion on you" (54:10). Though these things happen,

Peace in the Pieces

what God has established cannot be removed. Friend, peace is not just a feeling we can rest in and find wholeness in; it is our portion. It is a place, a spiritual one not confined by four walls, that is laid down by God for us to dwell with Him. You see, Jesus promises His people peace through the third person of the Trinity—the Holy Spirit—in Galatians 5, but Jesus, too, is a person of peace. Isaiah 9:6 makes it clear that Christ is the Prince of peace, the Ruler of peace, the Author of peace, the Distributor of peace, and the Source of our peace. All in all, our God is all about peace! Every piece and part of His personhood is peace.

There were times when I tried to find peace in my life through other meaningless things. I tried to find peace and assurance through the approval of others, but that only caused more striving and anxiety within me. There are people in our world who are trying to find peace in crystals and the New Age, but it's only inviting more darkness into their lives. I have friends who believe that their peace will come from a paycheck, but that doesn't quiet the storms in their hearts.

Maybe for you today, you have sought peace from painkillers and substances, but it's only a Band-Aid and isn't getting at the root of your hurt. Maybe you've tried to find peace in online shopping, but it's only deepened the debt and depression in your life. Or maybe you've tried to find peace in binging your favorite shows or foods, but you only end up feeling unsatisfied and emptier than you imagined possible. Friend, Jesus brings full and complete peace. Full and complete healing. Full and complete wholeness. Full and complete restoration. He not only *gives* us internal peace, but He *is* our eternal peace.

God gifts us peace. We can receive this gift today and be blessed with calmness, security, and order in any area of struggle, strife, or stress. I believe that God will give you peace as you visit your unstable family on summer break from school. That God will give you peace as you await the ambiguous meeting with your supervisor that randomly appeared on your calendar. That God will give you peace as you navigate the sudden loss of a friendship or loved one. That God will give you peace as you figure out how to deliver the bad news you haven't yet been able to process yourself. That God will give you peace as you surrender the aspirations you invested so much time and effort into for His plans over your life. God's peace interrupts and pushes out the waves that are flooding your sinking ship, bringing it to a stillness and calm in uncertain waters. He is who we can be certain of no matter what.

Shalom in the Storm

There have been times when I felt like I was living life in the eye of a tornado, and somehow, God was keeping me safe, grounded, and at peace. I mean that literally. I survived a crazy tornado that swept through Dallas, Texas, back in 2019, and it was because of God. The concrete building I lived in shook profusely. I was all alone, tucked away in my closet, covered in pillows and bedding, praying that God would spare me as sirens wailed and the lights cut out.

Then suddenly, like one of the many blankets that covered me, I felt peace wrap me in a comforting swaddle. Something deep down inside me knew I was going to be okay. Whether I was knocked down by the tornado and about to meet my Maker face-to-face or my building and I remained untouched, I knew I had the Lord and that I would be okay. Thunderous roars began to echo in the hallways outside, and then ... stillness. The building stopped shaking, the howling winds silenced, and I calmly fell asleep under my coat.

I found out the following morning that the building beside me, a giant hardware store, had been destroyed. I am talking decimated. Completely ripped apart and scattered all over the ground. It was as if it had never been there. Thank God there were no people in there when it happened because it was a bone-chilling sight. The first thing I thought was how that was almost me and all the residents in my building, but the second thought that quickly followed was to praise God for His peace and protection in all that havoc.

I know what it's like to feel the peace and protection of God in those places, literally and spiritually: from tornadoes, to talking myself down from anxious spirals, to managing my household when my mother had another relapse or big binge. I did everything Philippians 4:6–7 said, and you know what? I experienced that exact peace! This passage says, "Don't worry about anything; instead, pray about everything. Tell God what you need, and thank him for all he has done. Then you will experience God's peace, which exceeds anything we can understand. His peace will guard your hearts and minds as you live in Christ Jesus" (NLT). By His grace, God guarded me physically that night the tornado ripped through, but He also gave me His shalom, His perfect peace, that guarded my heart and mind so that I could sleep in the middle of the storm. That is the kind of peace that only God can give. A peace that sends you to sleep in a storm, unfazed and completely calm, just like Jesus on the boat.

When I went to Israel back in 2018, the only souvenir I brought home with me was a ring that I had customized with Psalm 46:10 etched on it in Hebrew. That verse reads, "He says, 'Be still, and know that I am God; I will be exalted among the nations, I will be exalted in the earth.'" That term for "be still," *raphah*, is a call to not just stop but to let go, to release, to loosen your grip, and to surrender your striving.[4] We can stop fighting to be in control, calculating the outcomes of our lives, and manipulating everything to go our way once we let go and cling to the reality that God is with us. He is our protector, provider, and perfect purveyor of peace. Once we know this, and trust that God is God and we are not, the peace that takes over us is freeing.

Whatever tornado you are in or sinking ship you climbed aboard, know that the God of peace is with you: before you, beside you, and all around you. The sovereign God of the universe, who is the Holy of Holies, has your best interest in mind. Not only that, He is the only One in complete control, and He wants your story to work out for your good and His glory. I don't know about you, but I am at peace knowing that this truth is true for me today and forever!

Chapter 10

JOY IN THE JOURNEY

What if I told you that I almost got a tattoo on my eighteenth birthday while stranded in Costa Rica with my church youth group after a volcano erupted and shut the whole country down?

That's a loaded question, I know! But there's no need to worry or judge me right off the bat. I didn't end up getting one—spoiler alert. And even if I had gotten one, remember what we just talked about earlier about context? That also applies to the Levitical laws, where we get the famous tattoo verse in Leviticus 19:28. This law addressed the pagan rituals of that time in which individuals cut and marked their bodies as part of worship to their idols and false gods.[1] God wanted His people to be set apart physically as well as spiritually given what that entailed during that culture and time. Regardless of this context, though, I'm pretty sure my mom would have killed me the second I got off the plane if I had come home with a tattoo after being trapped in a foreign country for a week longer than she had anticipated.

Instead of boarding our flight when we were supposed to, we were chilling on the beach while our pastor and trip leaders were frantically figuring out how and when we'd be getting home. While I was downing a slice of pizza, I saw a random tattoo shop across the street and got the bright idea that maybe I'd pop in since the leaders were busy calling the pastors and parents back home. Clearly my eighteen-year-old angst was kicking in. I wanted to do something significant to mark my transition to adulthood—something symbolic. Something permanent, perhaps! I reasoned that getting a tattoo in a country I had never been to, where I didn't speak the language, would be perfect.

Now, rewind it back to the year 2015 when everyone was getting tattoos of infinity signs, feathers, elephants, tiny mustaches, bows and arrows, and the words *live, laugh, love* on their rib cages unironically. This was the era when indie folk was at its peak, "Thrift Shop" by Macklemore and the "Harlem Shake" were sweeping the culture by storm, and Coachella was in its prime. In a time of some of the most memorable and cringeworthy tattoos (no offense if you have one, because that is truly an iconic period piece), I just wanted a simple tattoo on my wrist in small font. In all caps,

I wanted the word *JOYFUL*. You might be rolling your eyes at me after I just knocked you down for your tattoo choices because mine sounds basic.

Really, Kirby? An eighteen-year-old Christian girl with a JOYFUL tattoo? Next you're going to tell me you have a tiny cross behind your ear and a little Christian fish on your ankle.

Before you call me basic, I have two things I want to say: (1) Needles scare me. So why on earth I considered a tattoo in the first place is beyond me. (2) This tattoo was more than just a cute phrase or permanent accessory that would live on my body forever. It was a word that served as a testament to who I was now in Christ.

I specifically wanted it on my left wrist because, for many years, that was the specific spot that marked my deep depression. Once etched and carved by razor blades in hopes of releasing the pain that was too much for a young me to unpack and shoulder alone, I wanted to mark it with a word of what God had done instead: the transformational work of bringing life from death, healing from pain, hope from sorrow, and joy from depression.

People are always caught off guard whenever I share that part of my testimony. The joyful, bubbly, Jesus-loving girl you see before you was once a suicidal, self-harming, hopeless trainwreck of a human who had no idea that God could take away the pain and bring healing to those hidden places. But despite my wrist not having that *JOYFUL* tattoo authored upon it (turns out my fear of needles won), my life does, and now the pages of this book do. There is a different type of ink serving as a testament to the joy, peace, hope, and healing that only Christ can bring when life eventually "lifes."

Yet I Will Rejoice

When your tapestry has been torn apart by the raging winds, it can be scary to allow yourself to fully feel joy. I've struggled with this too. I know that feeling joyful feels risky because it hurts to lose it. It's a very vulnerable emotion to fully embrace. If you've lost joy before, then you know what I'm talking about. Maybe you are afraid to get to that place of contentment, happiness, and liveliness because you're anxiously awaiting disappointment to knock at your door again.

For the sake of protecting my heart from breaking—or at least trying to—there were times when I allowed cynicism to creep in, negative perspectives to take over, and low expectations to be the bar so that I wouldn't get my hopes up and lose more joy. Instead of placing my joy in Jesus and my hope in God's personhood, promises, patterns, and presence, I've had seasons when I tried to find my joy in other people, possessions, power, and platforms where I felt like it was less of a risk. Maybe it's because I was under the illusion that if I placed my joy in all these other things, I would be able to control and manufacture it, whereas with God, the elements of surrender, trust, waiting, and hoping are at play.

Our joy does not come from other people, other *broken* people. Our joy isn't based on opportunities or expectations either. Neither is our joy contingent on the outcome of our best days or the worst-case scenarios. Friend, our joy should come only from the Lord. That's the *only* source of true joy. It's easy to praise God when the sun is shining and the grass is green. It's harder to believe the truth that God is good when it's blizzarding, hailing, and the winds are knocking over your fence. But the joy of the believer isn't set on circumstances; it's set on the truth of who Christ is in our highs and our lows because He is unchanging. Remember, He is that sugar that makes our lemons into lemonade! It is in Him, His presence, and His faithfulness that there is fullness of joy (Psalm 16:11).

> The joy of the believer isn't set on circumstances; it's set on the truth of who Christ is in our highs and our lows because He is unchanging.

Consider It Pure Joy

James has always been one of my favorite books of the Bible. It was the first book of the Bible that I ever studied when I got saved—the same summer my life hit the fan. My closest friendship had ended, my mother relapsed into alcoholism after years of sobriety, and because of my faith, some people began to criticize me and ostracize me; it was not the most fun lineup for a girl entering her freshman year of high school.

But here is where the book of James came in. In James 1:2–4, Jesus' half brother wrote to his readers, "Consider it pure joy, my brothers and sisters, whenever you face trials of many kinds, because you know that the testing of your faith produces perseverance. Let perseverance finish its work so that you may be mature and complete, not lacking anything." Can we just let those first four words sink in? *Consider it pure joy.* What exactly? Our *suffering.* The various trials of life. The pain. The unfair moments. The out-of-control storms that don't come knocking but barge through our front doors. The only reason joy can coexist with the difficulties of life is because of our hope in our Redeemer, Jesus. This is the point James was making.

I remember being locked away in my room, isolating myself from my mom after she got into another drunken scream-off with me, tears gushing out of my eyes, staining my thin Bible pages, and reading those exact words.

Really, God? This suffering I am living in is supposed to be joyful? Make it make sense! There is nothing joyful about this. If anything, this feels like a nightmare. This feels like hell.

Rather than slamming my Bible shut, shaking an angry fist at God, and finding something to distract me from the questions and the pain, I decided to do something different. I decided to dig deeper.

Okay, God. If this is what I am supposed to do, teach me how to do it.

The first command James gave us through the Holy Spirit's inspiration is to *consider*. When we consider something or are considerate of a situation, we take time to evaluate what it is or what it means. Rather than jumping to conclusions or responding on impulse, we pause, collect ourselves, root ourselves in Christ, pray for His wisdom and insight, and evaluate it through the lens of truth.

Perhaps instead of thinking about how God is using this for your demise, you can consider that God may be using your season and circumstance for your own character growth, spiritual maturity, and for a greater good you haven't yet thought of. I believe that God wants to develop in all of us a new attitude and perspective toward the trials that we will face. This doesn't demean or minimize the realities of pain and suffering, but it does give us hope to overcome what would have otherwise overtaken us. Instead of tossing us around like reckless waves, the command to "consider" stills us so we can see Jesus and confidently stand on the waves with Him.

I'm not going to gaslight you into thinking your trauma is no big deal or deny that the trials suck. To be honest, I don't get excited when I find myself in times of trouble. I am no Paul McCartney, all right? Sometimes it's hard to let it be! There have been times in my life when I've been discouraged, knocked down, and fed up, especially when it felt like day after day, nothing was getting better. But as I have matured in Christ and meditated on the words of James here, I am absolutely sure that joy can coexist in those moments. Not only that, it should be the essence and foundation we build hope on when hardship comes.

We can consider it *all* a joy—not just parts of it but every ounce of suffering we go through. How is this possible? It's because we know that there is endless potential for God to repurpose it for something greater. I am talking about redemption, friend! Not only are there infinite possibilities for God's redemptive power to be at work, but the fruit that comes from trials is of great worth.

The Fruit of Perseverance

The first fruit that suffering produces within us is perseverance. When I think of a person of perseverance, I think of the person who gets back up no matter how many times they fall or fail, just like Proverbs 24:16 speaks of. My favorite childhood movies, like *Finding Nemo* and *Meet the Robinsons*, taught me to "just keep swimming" and keep moving forward when life gets tough, but they aren't the only stories that affirm this. The great big story of the Bible does too! Our trials are never a waste of time. In fact, they are a prime place for us to grow in godly character and perseverance.

So many people I look up to are who they are because of what they have endured and persevered through. They embraced whatever came their way, called upon the Lord to repurpose it, and came out the other end refined. Each of them saw the treasure that was hidden within perseverance—the treasure of character development, solidified faith, and deeply rooted hope. These are the things that withstand time. With Christ, perseverance sanctifies us and forms us into who God has called and created us to be. Just as

Romans 8:28–29 says, "And we know that in all things God works for the good of those who love him, who have been called according to his purpose. For those God foreknew he also predestined to be conformed to the image of his Son, that he might be the firstborn among many brothers and sisters." Perseverance and the trials we face don't need to push us back; they can propel us forward into the identity we have in Him.

The best part is that God has given us everything we need to run the race well and endure the long journey of life. He has given us access to a relationship with His Holy Spirit and also His Word to cling to when life hurls ninja stars at our beautiful tapestries. Romans 15:4–6 says, "For everything that was written in the past was written to teach us, so that through the endurance taught in the Scriptures and the encouragement they provide we might have hope. May the God who gives endurance and encouragement give you the same attitude of mind toward each other that Christ Jesus had, so that with one mind and one voice you may glorify the God and Father of our Lord Jesus Christ."

We can have hope and joy that He will knit us together and fashion our stories to have a greater impact than we could imagine. There may be a time when we just sit with Him in the ashes, marking our Bible pages with tears, but there will also be a time when He gives us what we need to get up, move forward, and persevere for a greater purpose—one that will be for the benefit of your life, the saving grace of other people's lives, and the greater glory of God's plans!

The Fruit of Spiritual Maturity

At the time this book is published, I will have been walking faithfully with Christ for fifteen years. I have spent more days doing life with Jesus than I have wandering alone without Him. If fourteen-year-old Kirby could see me now, she would be jumping for joy! But I didn't stay surface-level with Jesus. Neither did I jump ship when the church camp highs wore off or good worship sessions ended. I stuck by Jesus, and He stuck by me. It was in the thick of the difficult moments and the stretching strides that my faith was tested and developed, proving itself to be true and Christ to be trustworthy. Suffering produces perseverance within us, yes, but it also develops spiritual maturity and strength that can withstand any season or storm.

On the spectrum of gym rat to couch potato, I am in the Pilates princess range. I don't sweat; I sparkle! But I recently started to incorporate more HIIT workouts and strength training into my routine. As I've researched it and incorporated more of those workouts into my weekly routine, I've learned that one of the best ways to build muscle is through resistance training. Resistance produces strength. But it's the way in which it makes your muscles grow that speaks to me spiritually.

I remember talking with one of the trainers at my gym, a five-foot blonde middle-aged woman who could easily throw me across the room if she wanted to. No joke, this woman's muscles are insane! One day after a weight training class she led, I chatted with her about how I knew I would be sore the next day from the workout she had led. After a chuckle, she explained to me that when stress is added to your muscles, microtears can begin to happen. Usually you start to feel the soreness and stiffness a few days later, but this is when your body begins to do something miraculous. Your body begins to repair and restore the tears, strengthening them so they can be more resilient and withstand more weight. Your muscles grow bigger, and so does your capacity for what you are able to resist and power through.[2] The stress and pressure are difficult, yes, but they are necessary for you to grow stronger.

In the same way, as we are stretched, tested, and experience resistance due to the lemons of life, with Christ, we can have joy knowing He rebuilds us to be stronger, more mature, and resilient in the face of pressure.

To be a disciple requires that we mature. The believer who desperately hungers and thirsts for Christ understands that suffering is part of our development. Through that process, we become more Christlike. The suffering we go through is also never in vain. Strangely and biblically, suffering is a joy (1 Peter 4:13), an honor (1 Peter 2:20), and a gateway to deeper intimacy with Christ (Philippians 3:10). I can honestly say the sweetest seasons of my life took place during suffering, which, from the world's perspective, would never make sense. But in those seasons, I encountered the loving embrace, the healing hand, and

> With Christ, we can have joy knowing He rebuilds us to be stronger, more mature, and resilient in the face of pressure.

the wise guidance of God so profoundly and clearly. I wouldn't trade what I learned and how I grew in those places spiritually and relationally with Christ for anything in the world.

We must accept the hard truth that without suffering, we will never fully arrive at the depths of spiritual maturity. We can either face life's trials with Jesus or without Him; they will come, but Jesus makes all the difference in our endurance of these trials. He makes them worth it. He brings resolution and redemption. He brings meaning and maturity to what we would've otherwise considered meaningless.

The Fruit of Completeness

Suffering, perseverance, and spiritual maturity lead to completeness— a believer lacking nothing. This is what James 1:2–4 declares! This should bring great joy to us as Christians, because isn't our aim to be more like Christ? To have fellowship with Him? To be sanctified by Him? In Him, we lack nothing! This truth is also penned in the Psalms by King David. He wrote in Psalm 23:1, "The LORD is my shepherd, I lack nothing."

When our suffering is met with faith in God, and we know who He is and how He works all things for good, we begin to develop maturity, wholeness, and completeness in Christ. The Greek word for "complete" used in James 1:4 is *holoklēros*. Though it translates to "whole," "without blemish or defect," and "flawless,"[3] I think another way we can look at this is *fullness*. We become full and complete people when we pass through suffering, embrace endurance, and learn the lessons Christ wants us to learn through spiritual maturity.

We gain so much in the trials: godly compassion, intimacy with Jesus, kingdom perspective, empathy for others, unshakable faith, lasting hope, and much more. We become full and complete people through suffering, and I think that is proof enough of God's redemption—that something as bad as suffering could be so good in the end.

It makes me think of the duality of the cross. What was meant for Christ's humiliation and torment was also the pathway for our salvation, forgiveness, and fellowship with Him. It was a form of suffering that Christ did not want to embrace yet also joyfully endured. On one hand, He pleaded with the Father to take this cup away from Him because He didn't want to face the wrath of God and the separation that the fullness of sin brings (Matthew 26:39). On the other hand, He also joyfully went to the cross knowing that this shame would lead to us being saved and reconciled back to Him (Hebrews 12:1–3).

Friend, you are the God of the universe's *greatest joy*.

When I realized that truth, I began to have a totally new outlook on suffering in my own life: suffering for the sake of the gospel, suffering the results of a broken world, and suffering the ridicule that comes from denying my flesh and taking up my own cross to follow Him. It all became worth it as *He* also became *my* joy.

The things we gain in suffering far outweigh the losses. Maybe the closed door to that ministry school you always dreamed of being a part of is crushing you now, but it's in the crushing that part of your character is developed for your calling. Maybe the burnout you're facing today after years of pouring out isn't the end of what God can do through you but the beginning of a restful season where God wants to deposit something new within you. Maybe the friendship that fell apart isn't a failure but a filtering—where God is making room for healthy community to step in and comparison to step out. Call me a broken record, but nothing is wasted when we submit it to God and invite Him to rewrite the story.

His Strength Is My Joy

Nehemiah 8:10 is where we get the saying "The joy of the LORD is my strength." But that's just the tail end of the whole verse. Do you know what the full verse actually says? It reads, "Go and enjoy choice food and sweet drinks, and send some to those who have nothing prepared. This day is holy to our Lord. Do not grieve, for the joy of the LORD is your strength."

Nehemiah, a historical book in the Old Testament, highlights a pivotal time in Israel's history when the exiles returned to Jerusalem. Upon arriving back, they began to rebuild the walls of the city and renewed their relationship with God. Once the walls were complete, Ezra, the priest and scribe, gathered God's people together to read God's law over them, which led them to weep and mourn over their deep conviction of sin.

I don't know if you've ever cracked open the Old Testament, but those Israelites were wild! It seems as though every other verse, they were back in some type of struggle—whether it was their own disobedience or the domino effect of humanity's brokenness against them. I find myself rolling my eyes and shaking my head at them, but truth be told, I am no perfect person either. Perhaps I should remove the log out of my own eye first before I start nitpicking the splinters in theirs. Anyways, back to the story!

Rather than sitting in grief and shame, Ezra, Nehemiah, and the Levites encouraged the people to celebrate because this was a holy day to the Lord. They encouraged them not to mourn, as we just read, but to find strength in God's joy. Godly joy enabled them to walk in grace, forgiveness, renewal, strength, and full relationship with their Lord and Savior. It was the joy of God's mercy and faithfulness to them that allowed them to rejoice and celebrate with gladness, and this is still true for us today. We can experience the joy of God because of the grace of God, the Word of God, the character of God, and through knowing God deeply and personally.

Some situations might make it seem like joy isn't available to us right now, but that is a lie. Wherever it is that you need joy today, trust that God will gladly give you His joy to endure, to hope, and to keep moving forward with purpose. You and I can have confident hope that God will renew our joy so we can move forward from past shame, fears, mistakes, and setbacks into a relationship with Him because of His grace. Friend, you've got Jesus; therefore, you've got access to joy!

Life with Jesus Is Everyday Joy

The Lord's joy is our strength, and we can only tap into that and experience that *daily* if we are communing with Him *daily*. Sure, I might be experiencing pain today, but I also haven't forgotten that, in other ways, I am living out the prayers I used to pray. I am grateful and recognize God's hand, will, and goodness in this season, even if there are trials or hardships in other areas of life.

The best part is that we get to actually know *Him*, because the gift isn't just joy itself; the gift is *God* Himself. If you want joy from the Lord, yes, you can pray about it. Yes, you can listen to worship music. Yes, you can go to a Christian summer camp. Yes, you can celebrate Him at Christmas at a candlelight service with your loved ones. But the thing is, all those things that bring us joy point to worship and communion with *God*. It is He who produces joy within us—not the timing, circumstance, or outcome. He is our joy and our strength when we say our amens, when the worship set wraps up, when camp pickup day arrives, and when the service ends.

If you are wondering how you can personally experience this kind of joy as God is still stitching together the rips and tears in your tapestry, allow me to offer some advice on where to begin. First, you do not have to fake your joy. You don't have to patch over your pain with smiles and shouts of "God is good!" Yes, He is, but you can be real about the areas where joy feels hard to come by. Every day, you can begin your day by inviting Christ into the spaces where it feels like His joy is lacking by simply saying, "Jesus, would You show up in this place in my life today? Would You grace me with Your hope, joy, and peace today?" It can be as simple as that. Simple prayers are not bad. Honest prayers are the best prayers in my opinion. And this can be a prayer prayed throughout the day as you read His Word, as you drop off the kids at school, as you fold your laundry, as you ride up the elevator to your meeting, as you mail out the invitations, as you hit Send on the lengthy email you were scared to type out. Invite Him in and ask Him to give you a portion of His joy today.

Another thing that has cultivated joy in my life is journaling. Buying the cute journal is sure to give me a quick dose of dopamine, but the real joy comes from writing down my complaints, laments, and problems to the Lord, as well as my prayers, thanksgiving, and gratitude for all that He has done in my life. I take time to pause and reflect on where I see God moving in my life, backing up the magnifying glass a bit so I can get the whole picture of how God is actively working in my life. This always leads to joy in my life, knowing that if He is working in all these other places in so many unique ways, then I can trust that He is doing the same behind the scenes with the things I worry over today.

A third way I always end up feeling full of joy is by cannon-balling into my Christian community! I am talking clothes-on, keys-in-the-pocket, spur-of-the-moment full send into the deep end with the people God has gifted me. Philippians 2:1–2 encourages us to be in this kind of community, saying, "Therefore if you have any encouragement from being united with Christ, if any comfort from his love, if any common sharing in the Spirit, if any tenderness and compassion, then make my joy complete by being like-minded, having the same love, being one in spirit and of one mind." The comfort of their love, the commonality of the Holy Spirit dwelling among us, and sharing the same kind of Christlike compassion is a recipe for joy. It's like your favorite warmed-up chocolate chip cookie! Joy can show up in the text messages from your bestie, the mentor meetings over coffee, and even the Bible study gatherings.

I encourage you to begin praying about who those people might be in your life. Whether it is a whole ocean of community or even a puddle of people, these consistent and caring voices who know, love, and serve God with all their hearts will give you the joy you need. And who knows, maybe you can be that friend to someone else praying the same prayer.

Questions and communion can coexist here. Tears and triumph can dwell together here. Pain and praise can be present at the same time here. When we welcome God into the darkest parts of our seasons, His joy begins to light up our lives and bring healing to the heartache. Even while the hurt still lingers, and even as you are still being made whole, His joy can still show up.

Chapter 11

EVERY WRONG MADE RIGHT

I'm not going to lie to you; there are some books of the Bible that I had definitely put off reading because I had no idea what was going on. Leviticus, with all the laws; 1 Chronicles with all the genealogies; and even Revelation, with all its apocalyptic language. But once I started pursuing my degrees in theology, I came to understand the context of those books, how to read them, and the beautiful purposes that they served to their original audience and to us today.

I especially loved diving into the book of Revelation, and now, when I think of it, I don't think of some crazy, futuristic sci-fi movie where I don't understand what's going on. I see the promises of redemption, restoration, and every wrong being made right by our awesome and powerful God—the One who wipes out evil with one hand (Exodus 15:6) and wipes away our tears with the other (Revelation 21:4). This is the future hope of heaven we can cling to!

Though there are unrealized things on this side of heaven, where sin, sickness, death, and disappointments still exist, that doesn't mean that God isn't redeeming things here and now. He is still a miracle-working God! We have hope for heaven, yes, but in Christ, we can also have hope for today, that His silver lining can lace up what's been unraveled. Take my friend Stefanie, for example. Her life shines with the Lord's silver-lined glory and grace, even in the painful parts that are still being woven together.

Stefanie is one of the purest and kindest souls I know. Both she and her husband, Caleb, help people unpack their relationship traumas and equip them to date and pursue relationships with a redeemed kingdom worldview. We need more of that in this confused and chaotic world we live in! They're also incredible friends to Richard and me, even across state lines. I wish they lived closer to us, so Stefanie and Caleb, if you're reading this, please move into the house next door to us! Sound good?

One thing I think everyone needs to know about Stefanie and Caleb is that they exude "world's best parents" energy. They are so attentive, nurturing, compassionate, and loving. I just know any child would win the family lottery if they ended up with them as their mom and dad! But sadly, after years of infertility, they still have yet to give birth to that blessing.

Not too long ago, there was a moment of hope for them both. After many years of praying, crying, and trying, they finally conceived—a true miracle! Life began to glimmer with color in an area that once felt abandoned and dull for them, hues of baby blue, to be exact! They praised the Lord for this child and couldn't wait to tell their friends and family after years of disappointments and negative tests.

But when they went for an early checkup, they were hit with the duality of the best news and worst news all at once. During the ultrasound, the sonographer looked at the screen, looked at Stefanie and Caleb, and looked back. "Did you know that you're carrying twins?" Twins! They did not have only one tiny miracle growing in her womb, but two! A set of perfect little boys were bundled up together, being knit and stitched by the Lord Himself. Tears of joy painted the floor of that doctor's office, but suddenly, they became floods of agony.

"We can't find a heartbeat on either of them. I'm sorry, but you've lost them . . . We have to get them out of you as soon as possible, or this could be fatal."

The words no parent wants to hear. The words no prayer warrior wants to hear. The words Stefanie and Caleb were never prepared to hear. As she recounted this journey to me, I wept with her. To have such a deep and pure desire in your heart given to you, then quickly taken away, is gut-wrenching. I know so many people who have walked through infertility, miscarriages, failed adoptions, prolonged singleness, separation, and all sorts of other avenues of disappointment in the family arena, and it breaks my heart each time. I remember asking her whether she questioned God at that moment. Did she waver in her belief? Did she doubt His goodness and faithfulness? Did she or Caleb forsake their faith because they went from barrenness to blessing, to double blessing, back to barrenness?

She told me that when they got home that day, instead of tearing apart their Bibles, throwing their crosses in the trash, and deleting "John 3:16" from their social media, they both got on their knees and worshiped God—not just worshiped Him, but *praised* Him through the tears.

I know that for many of you, your immediate reaction to having your world come crashing down is not to raise your hallelujahs. I don't blame you. You are no less of a "good Christian" if you sit in your sorrows. I mean, look at the Bible! Plenty of people put on their sackcloth, covered themselves in ashes, and lamented for days, weeks, months, even years over the loss and grief of life's changes and disappointments (Genesis 37:34; Esther 4:1–3; 2 Samuel 1:11–12; Nehemiah 9:1).

To grieve is to be human. I know we think that the book of Psalms is all about praise, but there is also a lot of lament in it. There is even a book in the Bible called Lamentations! It is human to sit in sorrow, and it is holy to sit in sorrow—to feel all those feelings and grieve what's been lost. But it is vital that we bring every tear before the Lord.

I love how Psalm 56:8 acknowledges this about God: "You keep track of all my sorrows. You have collected all my tears in your bottle. You have recorded each one in your book" (NLT). God knows every tear you have cried, friend. You don't have to hide them and act like everything is fine when it's all falling apart. Stefanie and Caleb weren't pretending anything. These incredibly faithful Christian people fully felt every ache, break, and pain, and yet they said, "Here, God. We give this to You and trust You. We trusted You at the beginning, and we will still trust You through this."

It's one thing to worship God because of who He is; it is a whole other thing to praise God for what He has done, for what He will do, and for what He will get you through—that whether it be in our lifetime or in heaven, all things will be right and redeemed. Even though they did not get the double portion they had prayed for, prepared for, and praised God for, Stefanie and Caleb continued to give glory to Him and trust Him in the loss, because they firmly believe to this day that He will use this for good, because He is good.

Stefanie isn't lying to herself and pretending that the questions don't pop up, or that this situation doesn't hurt. It does hurt. However, God's character as a healer, comforter, restorer, and redeemer remains unchanged. He is the constant who is consistently faithful, true, and unwavering, even when our broken world unravels and we fall into unexpected sorrow. For the mamas and fathers out there who have gone through the loss of a child, who didn't get the adoption at the last second, or who have struggled with infertility, I am so sorry. Children are a blessing, and I know there are probably a million questions and doubts swarming through your mind at all times whenever you dwell on this. But let me remind you that, when things don't go our way—and this goes for everyone—God can still redeem it for something good. This is our hope, the confident assurance we cling to.

Sometimes that looks like the return and restoration of what was taken from us; other times it looks like God repositioning us and repurposing our sorrow to be a story of His glory. Regardless, we can grieve with hope, endure hardship with hope, and cry all the tears with hope, knowing that when we bring our disappointments, messes, laments, and praises to Him, He receives them, He receives us, and He begins to do a good, redemptive work in our hearts. This is the heart and the hope of the gospel: not just forgiveness and fellowship with God but the redemption of God's people to Him—the vision of our broken world inching toward a new heaven and a new earth (Isaiah 65; Revelation 21).

When the Worthy Are in Waiting

In John 9:1–7, we are introduced to a man who was born blind. Jesus and His disciples came across this guy, and the disciples asked Jesus, "Rabbi, who sinned, this man or his parents, that he was born blind?" (v. 2). Here is Jesus' response in verses 3–5: "Neither this man nor his parents sinned . . . but this happened so that the works of God might be displayed in him. As long as it is day, we must do the works of him who sent me. Night is coming, when no one can work. While I am in the world, I am the light of the world."

You see, the disciples lived in a culture where a person's suffering was assumed to be tied to the person's direct sins against God.

Yes, our personal involvement in sin can open doors of suffering for us, but the original sins of Adam and Eve opened the door for suffering in the world, *period*. It might not be a direct result of *your* sin but humanity's sinful state, and if I know one thing to be true about Jesus, it is that He redeems all things.

He redeems sin.

He redeems brokenness.

He redeems disorder.

He redeems barrenness in more ways than one: emptiness in the wombs of real people, yes, but also emptiness in our lives where hope never seemed possible. The barren seasons of wandering, the barren dreams we've pursued, and even the barren answers to prayers we've prayed. But the truth is that each pause that felt empty was only a moment of God silently moving, working, and redirecting things to be attuned to the perfect will and plans He has for your life.

> Each pause that felt empty was only a moment of God silently moving, working, and redirecting things to be attuned to the perfect will and plans He has for your life.

Barrenness can feel like a complete wilderness, I know, but the wilderness is not the same thing as a wasteland. Why? Because nothing is a waste to God. Often, as we see in Scripture, God's Holy Spirit leads us gently, closely, and intentionally into these spaces and seasons for a reason far greater and far more glorious, so that we can do far greater and far more glorious things with Him.

This story is still being written for Stefanie and Caleb, but one perfect example of a story with its conclusion already written is the story of Jesus' relative, Elizabeth.

You know when you open up your Bible and God starts speaking so clearly to you just from the first few verses alone? Yeah, that was me with Luke 1! When I got to Luke 1:5–7, I couldn't help but reread it, and reread it, and reread it: "In the days of Herod, king of Judea, there was a priest named Zechariah, of the division of Abijah. And he had a wife from the daughters of Aaron, and her name was Elizabeth. And they were both righteous before God, walking blamelessly in all the commandments and statutes of the Lord. But they had no child, because Elizabeth was barren, and both were advanced in years" (ESV).

Elizabeth was a relative of Mary, a.k.a. the mother of Jesus, and—spoiler alert—the mother to John the Baptist, the forerunner of Christ who prepared the hearts of the people to repent and believe in their coming Savior. What a family! I can only imagine that when Jesus showed up to His family holiday gatherings, which I know must have been often given all the festivals celebrated in the Jewish culture, John the Baptist would have been the coolest cousin at the kids' table. He was probably munching on honey and locusts, freaking out all the other cousins and siblings while Jesus laughed it off. But take notice of Elizabeth and her husband, Zechariah; he was a priest who performed sacred duties in the temple, and they were both deemed righteous people who lived blameless, obedient lives to God—yet they were barren.

Barrenness was seen as a curse to the Israelite people. Christian scholars have stated, "The image of the barren wife is one of the Bible's strongest images of desolation and rejection."[1] Knowing that children were valued and interpreted by the Israelite people as a sign of God's blessing, favor, and covenantal faithfulness, this point of view makes sense. But here is where that POV doesn't add up: Elizabeth.

She was a righteous woman, meaning she lived rightly before God, honoring His commands and authority. She was a blameless woman, not delighting in sin and having no notable record of wrongs. She also obeyed the statutes and commands, valuing God's laws and society's order. And to top it all off, her husband was a priest! Her barrenness, in the eyes of the culture's standards and the spiritual interpretation of her society, didn't make sense. It didn't make sense for someone so worthy to go through the waiting.

Maybe there is an area of your life where you've been waiting on God with hope and expectation, but it hasn't yet happened. Maybe, like Elizabeth, or my friend Stefanie, you've been obedient. You've been faithful. You've loved the Lord, served Him and His people greatly, and trusted, waited, and prayed, and you are wondering why it hasn't happened for you yet. Or worse, maybe you came close to receiving the very thing you've hoped for, only for it to feel "taken away" by God at the very last second. For being so kind, maybe you've felt like that was the cruelest thing God could have done to you.

Whether the thing you're praying for and requesting from God will or won't happen is not my claim to make, but here is what I do know: Delay isn't the same thing as denial. I know I already spoke to this in an earlier chapter, but it's worth repeating. Just because God is silent on something doesn't mean He won't speak to it. Just because He hasn't entrusted something to you doesn't mean you did something wrong and are unworthy in God's eyes. I don't know what words society spoke over you or Pharisee-like Christians cast toward you, but I can only imagine the words that Elizabeth heard as people tried to comprehend what didn't make sense.

The tension between faith and frustration is a hard place to hold it all together, I know. But I want you to know that, on the days when you feel tired, torn, and worn out, and are wondering why you still trust in God and His plans, He is still holding you together. You can let go, lament, and place these things to be purposed in God's gentle hands.

I can't promise you that you will get everything you pray for, and that it will arrive tomorrow just like your Amazon Prime order will. But I can promise you, because God has promised it, that your waiting isn't wasted and His love for you isn't measured by what you do or do not receive, or when you do or do not receive it (Lamentations 3:25–26; Psalm 103:10–11). He also promises that He is near to us when our hearts are shattered (Psalm 34:18), that the tears we cry will bear the fruit of joy in our lives (Psalm 126:5), and that He will complete a good work in our lives (Philippians 1:6), even if it is slower than we expected and paved with a path of unknowns.

When Barrenness Leads to Blessing

Barrenness is an opportunity for a bigger blessing of redemption to be ushered in by God. As much as this relates to the literal wombs of people, I also know there are people who will pick up this book and have aspects of their life that feel empty and decimated by the grief of giving and taking away. So please know this also applies to you if that is your reality today. Barrenness wasn't seen as a blessing by the ancient Israelite society, but in these divine moments in the lives of faithful people, God brought about redemption and blessing that impacted families—even nations! Not just a singular individual but hundreds and thousands around them. John was not just a blessing to Elizabeth; ultimately, he was a blessing to Jesus, *to God.*

What if the barren area of your life, that space that feels open and empty or lifeless and useless, was the perfect opening to be occupied by God's plans and purposes for redemption and greater glory? What if, in His timing and in trusting Him, we could dare to hope that, by whatever means, in whatever way, and for whatever reason, God could use this for a bigger purpose and for more than just us? For more than just our limited expectations and dreams? This hypes me up with so much hope, because I know, looking back upon the places that were once barren in my own life that are now full and fulfilled, that God has worked everything out! I can dare to have hope in this because He has already proven Himself faithful.

> I can dare to have hope in this because He has already proven Himself faithful.

When Elizabeth was barren, she continued to live righteously before God, trusting in His plans and purposes even before she was blessed with her baby. What if we dared to do that too? Amid our places of depravity, of discomfort, of unmet dreams and expectations, we could allow God to fill that void, to take up occupancy in that empty room, and let Him set up shop to do something wonderful where we were convinced initially that it was wasted.

What if we chose to believe in the reality of God's redemption rather than the narrative that we will forever be stuck in grief, disappointment, and frustration? That there is no hope for this place? Because the truth is that Christ is our Redeemer (Isaiah 63:16; Ephesians 1:7)! It is His will, His way, and His nature in all He does and all He allows. What that will look like specifically, I am unsure, but that's where the excitement and wonder kick in, remember?

Eventually, God sent an angel to deliver a message to Zechariah, Elizabeth's husband, as he was faithfully serving in the temple. This is what the angel told him in Luke 1:13–15: "Do not be afraid, Zechariah, for your prayer has been heard, and your wife Elizabeth will bear you a son, and you shall call his name John. And you will have joy and gladness, and many will rejoice at his birth, for he will be great before the Lord" (ESV).

When entrusted to God, a barren place bears a blessing. This trust marked Elizabeth's and Zechariah's entire lives, and God honored that, even when they lived their lives not expecting anything from God in return. Whether they got the "blessing" they dreamed of or not, they knew who the ultimate blessing was—God Himself. And being the good Father He is to us children, we can trust that whatever blessing He brings us, whether it is on our registry or not, it will have a beautiful, fulfilling, and redemptive purpose. For Elizabeth and Zechariah, it was John. Who knows what it could be for you.

Regifting and Repurposing the Pain

Fine. I'll admit it. I have definitely received a gift I didn't like before, pretended like it was the best thing I ever could have gotten, and then immediately set it to the side once I got home so that I could regift it at the perfect time. It's kind of like the five-second rule; you have to wait it out a little bit before regifting a gift. You have to hang tight for the right person or the right circumstance to come along. Just make sure whoever gave the gift to you in the first place isn't showing up to that event! Maybe I'm the villain for doing that, but you would do it, too, if you got someone a nice, intentional gift and all you got was a pair of used men's socks (true story). Are you starting to empathize with me now?

Sometimes there are things we can beautifully repackage and gift to someone else so they can find real purpose in what you were given. This way of thinking doesn't just have to be limited to the crummy white-elephant gift you got stuck with or the birthday present your relative gave you that you have to keep on display until they go back home after the holiday drop-in. With God, we can take a new look at the things life handed us, and He can repackage them so they can give purpose to other people's pain.

Here is the thing: As much as God can move in your mess, tend to what's been torn, speak to you in the storm, fasten what's been frayed, and shape your character in the cracks of life, He can also repurpose it for the good of others. I think a perfect example of this is this book right here.

Part of me thinks about all the seasons of heartache, disappointment, grief, and trauma I went through, and I wish they didn't happen. I think of four-year-old Kirby, when she was exposed to images she never should have seen; seven-year-old Kirby, whose parents were divorced; ten-year-old Kirby, whose dad died days before he was supposed to fly in and visit; thirteen-year-old Kirby, who was bullied and planned to kill herself; fourteen-year-old Kirby, whose mom severely relapsed after she got saved; eighteen-year-old Kirby, whose boyfriend betrayed her behind her back by living a double life; nineteen-year-old Kirby, who was sexually assaulted by two different guys over the course of a few months, and who carried so much shame and fear because of that; twenty-three-year-old Kirby, who lost all her community and job opportunities when a worldwide pandemic shut everything down; and twenty-six-year-old Kirby, whose mom died tragically and traumatically in the ICU a few days after Mother's Day. As much as I wish I could have prevented all of these things, I see how God has used them for so much more than I ever could have thought or dreamed possible.

As I have matured in my faith and been molded into the person I am today because of those trials, I am now grateful that I went through them with God and have this testimony of hope that can be passed on to others. I know this also might sound weird, but there is a part of me that is thankful for each hardship I've been able to overcome—*overcome* being the key word there.

Like a baton in a relay race, I get to pass on to you, grieving your loved one perhaps, the hope that I've been able to experience in Christ. I get to hand over to you, confused why the dream didn't work out on your timeline, the peace I've been able to experience in Christ. I get to transfer to you, drowning in defeat and depression, the joy I've been able to experience in Christ. I get to share with you, sitting in the ashes of what has been burned up in your life, the redemption that has been promised to each of us who knows Christ the Redeemer. Consider this blatant honesty as my gift to you: If I was able to get through all of this stuff and still stand with an assured hope in a real and good God, then there is hope for you as well.

Redemption Beyond Our Perception

Thrift shopping has become super popular in recent years, which makes me laugh as I look at the correlation of my generation and the economy we are in. We Gen Zs and millennials know how to make lemonade out of lemons, all right, because it's not high-end fashion that's trendy and exclusive anymore; it's rocking someone's great-grandparent's clothes. That mothball-smelling cardigan I'm wearing? Yeah, it's one of a kind. I call it the penny-pincher special!

But as much as we can be thrifty and repurpose the things given to us, I think God is the ultimate thrifter! He takes the things we have gone through—the scuffed-up, loose-threaded, button-missing moments of our lives—and restores, renews, and repurposes them as a gift to us and as a gift to others. The fabrics we would have tossed in the bin are now being restitched and recycled as an original piece we get to show off. From rags to riches, He breathes new life into us and our stories, adding immense value to the seasons we've walked through.

Sometimes the redemption that is coming is beyond our perception. Maybe our gaze has been fixated on the broken pieces more than the hands of the One who can mend them. Maybe our vision has been blurred by our welling tears. Can I encourage you today to set down the remains of whatever you've been holding on to and fighting to glue together, and to look ahead at where God is calling you to step out and trust Him? To place the broken things into His hands to be made new? In the book of Isaiah, we get this beautiful declaration to behold in chapter 43, verse 19: "See, I am doing a new thing! Now it springs up; do you not perceive it? I am making a way in the wilderness and streams in the wasteland."

God is doing a new thing, and He is inviting us to behold it. To be still and begin sowing the things that have been torn and fragmented in our lives into the Savior's soil. There, it will slowly but surely begin to take root, and with the right combination of soil, water, and sunshine, the fruit that will come out of it will be unlike anything you ever tasted—so much sweeter than the lemons we created!

Friend, it is time for new things to grow in your life, and that requires a sowing and a sewing. Remember that God is the most trustworthy person we could partner with in this cultivating work, and the sooner we can believe that about Him, the quicker we can step into the story of redemption He's already been working on for you and me.

Chapter 12

WHAT IF GOD DOESN'T DO IT?

I know what you're thinking. *Kirby, what now? I am still barren despite walking blamelessly, living faithfully for God, and trusting in His timing and plan. I am still suffering even though I have faith that God can heal and is true to His character. Will it ever be my time? Will He ever deliver me from this lot in life, this lemon I'm forced to squeeze? Everyone thinks I'm a fool, and I'm starting to think that about myself as well. What if it never happens for me? What if God doesn't give me the blessing I'm hoping for?*

First of all, take a deep breath and let it out slowly. I understand this can hit some sensitive nerves, some bitter wounds, some painful bruises, and even reopen some scarred places you've slapped a Band-Aid over and tried to power through. The daunting anxiety of what-ifs can be debilitating and defeating. The waiting can feel wishful and worrisome when days have gone by and redemption hasn't panned out how you expected or on your timeline. But I want to give you four practical things you can do today to help you if you are finding yourself spiraling in fear, doubt, and anxiety over God's perfect plans and timing in your story.

1. Move from What-If to Even-If

I tend to spiral when things get overwhelming. One thought leads to another, and before I know it, I've lost track of time and lost my mind. I have anticipatory anxiety and panic over potential outcomes years down the line. My mind jumps from *What if I don't get the call back?* all the way to *They must hate me, and they're going to tell everyone else they hate me, and because of that, I'm never going to get booked for anything and my life is over!* I really do go jumping from zero to one hundred real quick. My prayer life looks a lot like me saying, "God, I'm trusting that You'll take care of these things because they are out of my control," but my actual actions look more like me wasting my whole day trying to map out a ten-year life plan so that I can make sure I get the exact result I want. I just know God is shaking His head in the most loving way at me with all my spiraling. He doesn't want me to get stuck in my mind. He wants me to live free and to live in full abandonment, trusting Him to do what He does best: be Lord over my life!

I know He wants nothing more than for me to trust Him and live at peace within His perfect plans and timing. If you are a fellow what-if-er like me, we need to get in the habit of "even-if-ing" instead. Even-if rests on the redemption of God, as well as His personhood, promises, patterns, and presence. It stands on the truth in a world of endless unknowns. Let me show you the mental dialogue I now have with myself as a recovering what-if-er:

What if my migraines are symptoms of some crazy brain tumor and I end up paralyzed and die!? Yes, this is an actual thought that I have to take captive because worst-case scenarios are my specialty as someone with an overactive imagination, I guess. But knowing the things that are true about Christ, I can take that thought and say to it, *Even if that were to become a reality, I know that my God is a healer, and even if He didn't heal me, God would use this to reach others who wouldn't otherwise be reached, and I would be one step closer to full healing in heaven.*

What if when I get older, my husband leaves me for some younger, skinnier, prettier girl, and then I am left all alone to take care of the kids and end up on the streets!? Richard has never given me any reason to believe that this would ever happen, because of his vows to God and to me, but the creativity that my trauma whips up never ceases to impress me and depress me.

I am blessed because every day Richard affirms his love for me, his commitment to me, and the vows he made to God when he married me, but that doesn't stop my mind from taking one silly thought and blowing it out of proportion like a big worrywart. If those thoughts rise within me and I sense insecurity and fear trying to manipulate me, I now respond with, *Even if that were to happen, God is my provider. He is my first love, and He will make sure that I and my hypothetical children are okay. And even if Richard were to ever leave me for those ridiculous reasons, I know my worth never stemmed from those things anyway. And just because another woman has those things doesn't mean she is more desirable or valuable than I am.*

What if I get cast on my favorite reality show, *Survivor*, and because I am a Christian, I get the villain edit, and then all of America hates me and uses me as an example to tear down the faith? You probably think I am clinically insane at this point. I have applied to be on that show six times now, and I plan on applying every time they have a casting call. Jeff Probst, if you are reading this, first of all, I pray that you would have the most life-giving relationship with Jesus ever! But second, please cast me on *Survivor*. Consider this submission number seven!

Whenever I think about how fun it would be to compete, I immediately start to spiral at the idea of how they would edit me to look like a villain, and how I wouldn't be able to handle all the criticism and ridicule. As someone who is a recovering people pleaser, I've had to remind myself, *Even if you were to get cast on a show, or gain fame for any reason, other people's opinions do not matter. You fear God, not man. Even if the world hates you for your beliefs, they hated Christ first, and He would uplift you with the strength, confidence, and support system you need to face any sort of manipulated backlash. Christ will fight on our behalf!*

I know those are just three examples, and some of them may seem silly, but taking my thoughts captive, like 2 Corinthians 10:5 says, separating my worries from reality, and de-escalating the what-ifs with the even-ifs, has protected my sanity and encouraged me to have hope no matter what comes my way. We need to know God's Word, store it in our hearts by meditating on it and memorizing it, and invite God into the places where panic rises within us, supplanting the what-ifs with even-ifs.

Here is what I want you to do—even you, Jeff Probst: I want you to make a list of every what-if that is rattling around in that beautiful mind of yours—every single worry and care. Before you go judging and shaming yourself or correcting it so it sounds Christian enough, just be honest about what your what-ifs are.

> Before you go judging and shaming yourself or correcting it so it sounds Christian enough, just be honest about what your what-ifs are.

Then, I want you to go one by one down your list, pray to the Lord over each of them as you read them out loud, and ask the Lord what is true about Him and His perfect promises, even if these things were to happen. Then, write out those truths instead. Maybe make a Father-daughter date out of it between you and the Lord and go to the craft store and make a whole poster to prop up in a place where you can read those truths every day, especially if they are things you constantly dwell on.

The Enemy does not have to have territory in your life or in your mind. God gave you the creativity and imagination you have to be used for His glory, not to keep you riddled with anxiety and fear. Invite Christ, our Redeemer, into your mind today to free up those thoughts with the hope and truth of who He is, even in the unknown!

2. Name It, Don't Numb It

Both of my parents were alcoholics, and they drank their problems away one bottle, box, or glass at a time. They numbed the pain, the fear, and the dread of their present sorrows and future worries rather than naming the things they were most scared of and scarred by. Silence wasn't their friend but rather their enemy, perpetuating an ongoing cycle of cover-ups, control issues, and coping mechanisms. At the root of their drinking problems was an even bigger issue: *pretending*.

Pretending that everything was okay, that they could do it all themselves, and that they didn't have any resentments or reservations when it came to how God allowed things to unfold in their lives. They pretended, and that led to pent-up anger, pent-up expectations, pent-up bitterness, pent-up questions, pent-up doubt, pent-up everything, and rather than confessing and naming these issues to God, they held it all in and held it against Him.

What If God Doesn't Do It?

What do you think would happen if our pretending ended and things got real? Some of us are afraid to go there because we know we are risking feeling real pain, maybe even further disappointment, which would require further numbing. But when we bring our real issues, complaints, and problems to God, He doesn't slap us upside the head for making a scene or expect us to get our act together. No, He heals the hurt. He provides the remedy and is the remedy, being the Great Physician (Mark 2:17). Where we may have medicated and numbed, God wants to come in and do real healing.

If I went to the doctor's office with a broken arm, a cut-up leg, and displaced ribs, and told the nurses that I was fine and just needed a Band-Aid for my leg, not only would they look at me funny, but I would also miss out on getting the full treatment and healing I needed. Sure, I could ask for medication to numb the pain, but there are some things that only spiritual surgery can fix. We need to make that divine appointment with God and name our ailments so that He can go in and run the labs and tests we need to pinpoint the problems and be made well.

In church, we emphasize the confession of sin so much, yet we forget to discuss the necessity of confessing the sorrows that are burdening our hearts as well. Even Jesus named His pain in the garden of Gethsemane and on the cross. You need to know that you are not weak for baring your soul and honestly sharing the things that are grieving you—the things you've been through, are going through, or are anticipating going through. You need to name your pain rather than numb it so that Jesus can bring you the healing and freedom you need to move forward in hope.

3. Get Still with the Stills

Remember how I talked about being still earlier? Well, I think we need to get still with the stills. What I mean by this is that even if we aren't seeing God do what we know He is capable of doing, we can still believe that He is good, able, and perfectly working out His will for our lives. When we go through tough times and life's lemons sucker punch us in the face, it's hard to reconcile the reality of who God claims to be. When times are uncertain, or when circumstances seem to contradict God, we must remain still with what is still true about who our God is.

God is still good.
God is still kind.
God is still working.
God is still on the throne.
God is still fighting unseen battles for us behind the scenes.
God is still loving.
God is still just.
God is still present.
God is still moving in our midst.

Which of those do you most need to believe today?

When life changes, our hope needs to be placed in God's unchanging character. I know it sometimes feels like the God of the Bible, who we read about, sing worship to, and pray to, doesn't translate to our pain and suffering, and you are not alone in that. Our situations scream one thing while Scripture states another. In the tossing and tugging of tension here, we need to be still and know who our God still is (Psalm 46:10). When we take a few steps back and remember the reality of who He is from our story's beginning and its end, we can have hope because He is still writing it. We are being redeemed by Him!

Relationship and remembrance are key to fueling a faith like this when what-ifs try to drown out hope in our lives. Remembering who God still is and reflecting on my own relationship with Him through the years and tears of my testimonies and triumphs, I have been able to get still, be sustained, and remain steadfast when life got rocky or I felt as though I went through a big patch of turbulence.

I was able to come out the other side, holding on to hope, and see the proof that He was still good. When silence lingered longer than I had hoped for, I stood still in the truth that God was still good to me, that He was still active and alive, and that He still speaks even through silence. Friend, it's time to call to remembrance that faithful record of who God still is, even when the storms come. I know that you might still be in the chaos, but you and I have confident hope in a God who doesn't change, who is still who He says He is.

4. Have an Attitude of Gratitude

When the earthquakes of what-ifs shake the ground I'm standing on, causing me to fall to my knees in fear of what could happen next, I have learned to posture myself in a position of gratitude instead of grumbling. Gratitude has been key to building real, long-lasting hope in my life. You see, gratitude shifts our perspective from the present problems, which are very real and that God genuinely cares about, to the other areas of our lives where God has proven Himself over and over. Gratitude reminds us of all that He has done and all that He has won—the victories against mental illnesses, the overcoming of addictions, the breakthrough with prayers for provision, and even the opportunities that launched us into our communities and callings.

Gratitude is an attitude I believe we all vitally need to adopt as believers if we are going to combat the dread and doom that what-ifs plague us with, because gratitude unlocks peace in our lives where we otherwise would have hyper-fixated, doubted, or abandoned God. When the spiral starts, it's easy to look at every single place where life isn't going according to our plans. This person isn't returning my texts, these bills went up too much, the new phone came out and I can't afford it, she got the promotion over me—and the list goes on. But how often do we back up and recount all the little miracles that God does in our daily lives? Once you start counting and weighing the blessings in your life, the little ones and the large, boy do they add up! Like being able to take a nice cold shower after pulling out the weeds from your lawn. Like when you turn on the radio and that one song that God has been using to minister to you is playing. Like when that one friend makes you belly laugh so hard you get an ab workout. Like being able to hug your spouse at the end of a long day and pray over each other before bed. These everyday moments of grace shouldn't go unaccounted for. We should be brought to a place of gratitude and thanksgiving for those little pockets of hope and God's grace that push us forward.

I don't say this to minimize your pain or to equate your very real struggles and requests with ungratefulness and complaining, but I am saying that we can bring our requests to God while also praising Him for all the other ways He has been faithful, merciful, and kind to us. We have so many unrecognized blessings that we should have gratitude for.

I know firsthand that grief and gratitude can coexist. It's an interesting duality to praise the Lord in your pain, to worship Him in your worry, and to trust Him in your trial, but it is not only possible; it is the rhythm of the lives of believers all throughout Scripture! The Psalms show this so candidly, especially in the life of King David. While some of the Psalms begin with raging anger, doubting questions, and raw laments, they triumph in songs of remembrance, gratitude, and thanksgiving. David wrote in Psalm 9:1–2, "I will give thanks to you, LORD, with all my heart; I will tell of all your wonderful deeds. I will be glad and rejoice in you; I will sing the praises of your name, O Most High." This is a declaration against despair and defeat—one that we are invited to join in on!

Our hearts need reminding that our God is still moving in so many areas of our lives. He has blessed us and shown us favor in so many different ways. Let's also not forget that He has answered prayers we forgot we even prayed.

What if we began to give God the worship and the praise right now for what has not yet happened? What if we gave Him thanks and showed Him gratitude in every circumstance, as

1 Thessalonians 5:18 speaks of? What if we did it right here, from this place of sorrow, suffering, grief, and groaning? Let's begin by thanking Him and expressing gratitude for what He has already done, what He is doing, and what we know He promises to do—for what is seen and unseen to us. I know that for me, with my own spiraling and worry, stepping into gratitude has been a surefire method to ignite hope within me where hopelessness once reigned.

God Is in the Glitter

I once heard in my grief journey that grief is like glitter. I know that makes grief sound shiny, shimmery, and splendid, but if you've ever seen a Mark Rober video where he confetti-bombs thieves who steal packages from people's porches, then you know that glitter gets everywhere and sticks to just about anything. I still find glitter on my clothes from my competitive cheer days decades later because we wore it everywhere, all the time! That's how grief, change, or any type of major loss can feel—like a huge glitter bomb that went all over the place and made what seems like an uncleanable mammoth of a mess. It takes time to work through it all and dust off what once seemed pristine. Eventually, as time passes, the heaps and piles of glitter appear to be more menacing than magical.

But the thing about glitter, which I already alluded to, is that it has a funny way of resurfacing. Maybe you move the metaphorical couch in your home one day, and out of nowhere, there glistens a speck of glitter. Maybe as you go through the clothes in your metaphorical closet to see what you want to keep, sell, and donate, one piece you tucked far in the back has some glitter fall off its cuff, leaving its sparkles all over your hands again. These little specks of glitter can be painful to remember and revisit. They can tug at the hope you have for healing over the hurt. I get it.

Glitter lingers. Grief lingers. Sometimes we have to live with the loss or change for the rest of our lives, and it will show up and stick to certain things we thought would pass with time. But glitter doesn't have to be a scary thing. Glitter can be a beautiful thing.

Those beautiful specks that feel more sorrowful than sparkling have this awesome ability: reflection. And at just the right angle, when we let the light of God in to shine upon them, what glistens and gleams off the glitter and grief are beams and flecks of His faithfulness. The loss and the longing are very real, very painful at times, and very valid, but they don't have to lord over your life. Jesus can lord over the grief that lingers, meeting us in the middle of the twinkles and tears, healing every heartache. We can reflect on His redemption, rescue, and relief. And my hope is that we can find a glimmer of hope that outshines the glitters of grief. Sometimes grief blinds us and causes us to stay stagnant rather than heal forward, even if that healing is slow and gentle.

> At just the right angle, when we let the light of God in to shine upon them, what glistens and gleams off the glitter and grief are beams and flecks of His faithfulness.

Life will continue to happen, and glitter will cause us to pause in the whirlwind of it all. But it doesn't have to crush you or derail you from the direction God is calling you toward, or from the pit He is carrying you out of. When that glitter gets in your eyes and the waterworks start to pour out, lift your gaze heavenward, knowing that He captures every tear in His bottle (Psalm 56:8 NLT) with the promise that one day, each one will be wiped away, and you will never weep again (Revelation 21:4). This is the hope of heaven. This is the promise of Christ. Even in the lows of our mourning and lamenting, we can sing praises and rejoice, knowing there is a greater redemption and hope awaiting us where what was once dead now has eternal life!

Hold on to Faith and Hope

One of my favorite John Piper quotes is, "God is always doing ten thousand things in your life, and you may be aware of three of them."[1] Looking back at the tapestry of my own life, where I can now feel and touch the stitches, patches, and silver threads God has sewn into it, I know this is true. We can trust that God is at work in our lives behind the scenes, even if we can't see how it's all coming together right now.

Whenever I read Scripture and see, from an outsider's point of view, all the details God was orchestrating within His people's lives and how it all came together, I get overwhelmed with a sense of peace, knowing that if He did that for them, He is also doing

What If God Doesn't Do It?

that for me. Maybe not in the same ways but in the way that best fits my story that He's writing. Friend, He cares about you and me. He cares about our stories. He is involved in every little detail. It's usually at the point when we "arrive" that we finally have an idea of why God did what He did, allowed what He allowed, took away what He took away, and changed what He changed.

What if, instead of experiencing that revelation upon arrival, we chose to have that hope and expectation now, knowing that we will have that outlook one day? Let's cling to hope, faith, and expectancy, but let's also allow the wonder and mysteries of God to have their way. Jesus told His disciples again and again that even though the crucifixion was coming, so was His resurrection. They had that hope and expectancy to cling to, even though they didn't have every detail as to what that resurrection and day of redemption would look like. There was still space for wonder to take place. There was still space for God to do what only He could do!

It's a strange duality to have expectancy and to also loosen the grip on expectation—to have conviction and yet to sometimes lack clarity. But that is the Christian walk, no? That element of faith we discussed earlier makes the story exciting! This lifestyle of partnering with God calls us to be still, to trust in God's workings, and to have confident hope through it all. We cannot reduce God to our timelines, our formulas, our agendas, and our methods. He is God—beyond and outside of our natural limitations and laws. His ways are higher than ours (Isaiah 55:8–9). If that is true, then so must be His redemptive plans for our lives.

Chapter 13

RESTITCHED, REPURPOSED, AND REWRITTEN

My husband and I have been able to go on some crazy trips together and make some incredible memories. When we went to Iceland, we trekked across one of the most insane glaciers. Bright, crystallized hues of blue and white met the black sands and green patches of moss. It was unlike anything I've ever seen; it was truly otherworldly! When we went to the islands of Hawaii, we snorkeled with turtles and fish one minute at the North Shore, then explored the rainbow tree forests off the Road to Hana the next.

The Fabric of Hope

When we went to New Zealand, we hiked a gigantic mountain that overlooked the beach where whales had made their way up the shore just days earlier, and as golden hour hit the coast, I lost my breath for the beauty of it all—and also because I was so out of shape and not prepared for that hike. I am not a cardio girly, all right? But for a view like that, I'm down for the climb! Miley Cyrus would be proud.

If you've ever hiked a mountain before, you know that the view from the summit is unbelievable. It's one of the most rewarding things ever! It's as if the second you make it to the top, you forget all about the struggles, challenges, breathing breaks, and body aches it took to get up there. You look back and laugh at yourself for almost quitting halfway through.

I know for me, there is always a point in the climb when I start to doubt whether it was ever a good idea. I dwell on my weaknesses, ruminate on my exhaustion, and overthink whether I will be able to finish. After all, I have some jacked-up knees from my cheerleading days and a displaced hip from a serious car accident. The climb isn't the most comfortable thing, but Miley didn't sing about that, now, did she? She could have at least included the gear I would need in the lyrics; I could have used the warning, girl! But here's the thing: That view always speaks for itself. Every valley, every trek, and every obstacle we get around is worth it for what awaits at the end of the climb.

> Every valley, every trek, and every obstacle we get around is worth it for what awaits at the end of the climb.

Like I said, one important part of hiking is making sure you have the right equipment with you. I am talking about the precious cargo that could aid you in your journey. But as we do life with Jesus, it is usually while we are on the journey that He starts to equip us with what we need for the next trail. Sure, we can go on the expedition loaded up with all the best backpacks, shoes, sweatshirts, and hiking sticks, but there will be twists and turns we weren't prepared for. Lucky for us, Jesus is prepared. In fact, He packs a few extra things for the hike so that you and I can finish this journey strong and make it to the destination He is leading us to.

There is cargo He adds to us while we hike, and simultaneously, there is cargo He calls for us to abandon to lighten our load to make the trip easier. Whatever He gives and whatever He asks us to surrender will always serve us best for what's ahead, because Jesus, our guide, has already gone before and prepared the way!

Precious Cargo Coming Through

One piece of cargo that we end up gaining as we hike through the valleys or make it up the mountain is the cargo of character development. I know that sounds like major main-character-energy lingo, but seriously! Think of any movie where the characters go on a quest. There is always a major inward transformation that takes place where the character is sharpened, pruned, developed, matured, and renewed along the way.

My husband and I are currently rewatching all the *Star Wars* movies with his youngest sisters, Emily and Rachel. What they don't know is that we are going to surprise them with their first trip to Galaxy's Edge at Disney after this, so shhh, don't tell them!

In the first three movies that came out in the *Star Wars* franchise,[1] we meet Luke Skywalker, a farm boy who just so happens to be a Jedi. The Jedi knights have this special bond with the Force, which can be used for good/light, or evil/darkness. Those who use it for evil, like Darth Vader (if you know, you know), are known as the Sith. Anyway, Luke did not have it easy. He was destined to fight Vader so that he could restore balance to the Force and bring order to the galaxy, but the reality is that if he were to have attempted that in the first movie, our farmer boy would have died instantly. It was the trials, the hardships, the training, and even the losses that molded Luke into the Jedi and man he needed to be to fight Darth Vader and triumph over the darkness with the light. That's the nutshell version of it, at least!

Similarly, sometimes God allows us to experience hardships in life in order for us to grow into the people we are called and created to be. It's those experiences that develop our empathy, our conviction for truth, our dependency on Christ, our humility, our gifts and talents, our reasoning and perspective, and so much more. We gain so much in the loss. This is also true for us in our relationship with Jesus. The Christian life is marked by the duality of loss and gain. We lose our lives by laying them down in submission to Jesus, surrendering and sacrificing everything for the sake of His name and glory. In that loss, which can be hard, we gain something so much greater: fellowship with God. We also gain purpose, identity, freedom, guidance, wisdom, joy, peace, hope, and unconditional love from Him. Following Jesus comes at a cost, but when we really count what we lose and what we gain, there is no question that He is worth so much more than any other thing we could cherish. He, and all He gives us, is the precious cargo!

In all my grief, sorrow, pain, and heartache, I have gained the greatest treasure: intimacy with Jesus. He shares in my suffering, empathizes with my pain, and strengthens me in my weaknesses. And the most beautiful part is that He gives me hope! Hope in who He is as a reconciler, redeemer, restorer, and renewer. I have seen this in the lives of my friends, I have read this in the stories of the Bible, and I have lived this personally. I hope you can believe that the same God of the Bible, the same God who restored me and gave me a hope and a future (Jeremiah 29:11), is the same God inviting you to trust and believe in His active and good work today. He is inviting you to follow Him through the valley and up the mountain. Will you say yes and take that first step to follow Him to wherever it is He leads you?

The Holy Calling of the Pioneer

While we are in the middle of climbing the mountain, going through its uncharted terrain and gasping for air because of the elevation, we aren't really thinking about what good can come from it other than the summit waiting for us. But the reality is that if God called us to climb the mountain, it's not just about us; it's also about those who will come behind us who have no idea where they need to step, where they need to rest, where they need to pivot, or where they need to scale. It's hard to climb the mountain, especially if you are the first to attempt it. It can seem so unfair, and it definitely feels harder without a paved path to follow, but the kingdom *needs* pioneers. Those young in their faith need your faithfulness.

Maybe you've been assigned or allowed to climb the mountain you're on because God put something specific in you to be able to trek it and help those who would otherwise give up or be lost. Maybe He gave you a banner of hope to carry to the top, stick in the ground, and claim that territory in Jesus' name!

Again, He repurposes the things we go through as a gift to us but also to the generations that come after us. I'm sure if you spoke about the climb you're on with other pioneers of the faith in your community, the generation that went before you would have so much advice and wisdom to pass down to you as you scale similar terrain. Maybe that's the lesson you need to embrace today: to share where you are with the pioneers who have gone before you so that they can offer you wisdom, encouragement, and hope for the journey ahead. Or maybe you are the pioneer, and you need to start proclaiming all that God has done in your life to champion those who are just about to start their expedition or who are at the cusp of reaching their summit!

This is the duty of the body of believers! First Thessalonians 5:11 commands, "Therefore encourage one another and build each other up, just as in fact you are doing." Likewise, Psalm 145:4 states, "Let each generation tell its children of your mighty acts; let them proclaim your power" (NLT).

Restitched, Repurposed, and Rewritten

The call to be a pioneer for God is a holy calling. It is a calling that God honors. I think one of the most explicit examples of this in the Bible is Abraham. He was chosen and called by God to be the father of the Jewish faith, from which our Messiah would descend, for both the Jew and the Gentile. The call of Abraham is detailed in Genesis 12:1–3, which reads, "The Lord had said to Abram, 'Go from your country, your people and your father's household to the land I will show you. I will make you into a great nation, and I will bless you; I will make your name great, and you will be a blessing. I will bless those who bless you, and whoever curses you I will curse; and all peoples on earth will be blessed through you.'"

This man had no idea where he was going. Scripture literally says that Abraham left and went to a place that he did not even know yet. He was the OG pioneer! But God was going to show him the way. Abraham's faithfulness to follow God and trust Him in this process resulted in blessings for so many generations, even up to us today.

Maybe the place that God is leading you toward doesn't seem clear, certain, or purposeful at this moment in time, but we can have confident hope that wherever God calls us to go, He goes before us. He is also faithful to honor and bless those who walk faithfully in His footsteps. Like a child stepping in the sandy footprints left behind by their father on the beach, so we are called to walk the pioneer walk in our Father's footsteps.

With that picture in mind, here is the best part about being called to pioneer: You might be called to go before others, but God pioneered the path before you. He went first. You are going second. Deuteronomy 31:8 encourages us with this as it reads, "Do not be afraid or discouraged, for the LORD will personally go ahead of you. He will be with you; he will neither fail you nor abandon you" (NLT). And again in Isaiah 45:2–3, the Lord declared, "I will go before you and will level the mountains; I will break down gates of bronze and cut through bars of iron. I will give you hidden treasures, riches stored in secret places, so that you may know that I am the LORD, the God of Israel, who summons you by name."

This is our God, friend! He calls us by name to the assignments He's given us and calls us to keep moving forward through the storms of life. He also goes before us up the mountain, and He also levels it out where it might be uneven, untraversable, and unknown. He is the factor that makes it doable, scalable, achievable, and beatable.

Whatever mountain it is you are climbing today, have you asked God to show you the path He's already paved for you to follow? Or have you been exerting all your energy trying to traverse an unknown environment apart from His leadership?

Don't do it on your own; do it with God. Do it His way! Follow His paths! Trust me when I say that He knows a lot more than any of us combined, and when it comes to navigating the wilderness, He has the best instruction and trail markers to follow. Remember that as you journey forward, He surrounds you. Psalm 125:2 promises us this, saying, "Just as the mountains surround Jerusalem, so the LORD surrounds his people, both now and forever" (NLT).

This may sound cliché, but you are not alone. There are plenty of people who have been where you've been. Not only that, but we serve the Suffering Servant, who knows what the deepest extents of suffering, betrayal, discomfort, rejection, and grief look like. We serve a Savior whose life and ministry were full of mountains—from the Mount of Temptation, to the Sermon on the Mount, to the mountain on which He was transfigured, to the Mount of Olives—Jesus has surveyed, scaled, succeeded, and suffered in this life too. The Bible says that Christ took upon Himself the entire wrath of God for our sake (Romans 5:9); that is a suffering that we believers will never, ever, have to endure because of His selflessness.

> Remember that as you journey forward, He surrounds you.

So hear me loud and clear when I say that whatever you're going through or have gone through, Jesus understands the pain, the questions, the fear, and every other feeling you're identifying with today more than anyone. And yet, His story ended in redemption. The cross didn't end with death but with life! Because His story did that, ours can too. That is the hope. That is the confident assurance we get to have when our faith is in Christ: that He gets it, that He gets us, and that He gets us through it. He isn't just waiting for you on the other side because He already went through it; He is right by your side, ready to walk this entire journey alongside you.

Walking out Faith Without Crutches

I have never broken a bone in my life until recently. In 2023, I was sitting at my dining room table, my legs twisted up like a pretzel on the chair, working with one hand on whatever emails I had to get through and using the other hand to shovel yogurt into my mouth. Obviously—with a spoon, not my hand.

After about thirty minutes of this, my spoon hit the bottom of the cup, and I took that as my sign to take a break, throw away my trash, and waste some time bugging my husband before I got to my next task. But here's the thing: That crisscross-applesauce posture I was sitting in caused one of my feet to fall asleep. There was literally no sensation in it at all! When I stood up to leave the room, instead of my foot landing normally on the ground, it limply and lifelessly plopped down on its side. Then it happened. I put all my weight on that sleepy foot, and suddenly, all I could focus on was the loud *snap* that echoed through my house. Anyone who saw my at-home security footage of it had a visceral reaction to the sound I heard firsthand.

To my surprise, I somehow managed to get myself onto the ground. I was poking and prodding at my numb foot, trying to shake it back awake from its backstabbing slumber. As the sensation returned, so did the pain. Immense pain!

Oh my goodness, what did I do to myself?!

It turns out that I fractured my fifth metatarsal and couldn't walk on it for a few weeks. I tried walking with crutches but gave up after a few days. Why did nobody tell me how painful it is to walk with crutches? I thought my foot was in pain, but my armpits? They needed their own type of treatment after trying to use crutches all day. They were so inconvenient, uncomfortable, and they always got in the way. Eventually, I had enough. I knew I couldn't handle another day on them, let alone a few weeks.

That's when a friend of mine generously got me a little scooter. It was bright green, had a little basket for all my things, and, best of all, it was *super* fast. I'd zip around my house playing the theme music from *Mario Kart* because that thing could rip and race around corners. My husband would even steal it from me and scoot around the house because it was so fun!

I eventually healed—kind of. To be honest, my foot still hurts a bit, but I guess that is just the luxury of getting old and letting something heal on its own. It's interesting how sometimes healing on our own versus going to the physician doesn't really restore us as we'd hope. I'm sure there is a sermon analogy in there somewhere, don't you think? But ever since that all happened, I've allowed friends and family members with foot injuries to borrow my scooter when they've gotten tired of their crutches, which, surprisingly, has been a lot of people.

I bring this up because I have heard many people call the Christian faith a crutch; you lean on it because you're broken, bruised, and have no strength to stand on your own. The scoffers insinuate that weak people need Jesus as a last resort, and strong people don't. They make fun of faith as if it were some delusional placebo we're all taking daily. Basically, they are calling faith a cop-out. But here's the thing about crutches: They are terrible! They made me feel more pain in more places, didn't do that great a job getting me from point A to point B, and I personally ended up tossing them because I knew I wasn't going to last on those things for six to eight weeks. Faith in Jesus, however, only causes me to feel peace where there was pain in my life. He's walked me through the trials of life with hope and joy, and has remained with me in the changing seasons thereafter. Faith is not a cop-out, crutch, or cliché; it is essential in order to endure, heal, hope, and thrive!

Here's the hard spoonful of reality that the world doesn't want to swallow: *We all have faith and hope in something.* For many people, they've placed their faith in themselves. Maybe you've even done that in the past and quickly realized that it didn't work out. Why? This is because, as finite human beings, we cannot make the world and its unraveling submit to our strength, control—or lack thereof—and orchestration. Some people put their hope in false idols or vices. I've seen people run to pick up a bottle instead of a Bible, thinking it will be the thing to support them, but it only debilitates them, depresses them, and drags them down into a deeper pit of desperation. I've seen people put their faith in the labels they've acquired and the success they've accumulated, only for life to burst in like a giant toddler, knocking down the Jenga tower they've built for themselves.

Here is why faith and hope in Jesus are different: He is the only firm foundation we can bet on to hold us up. Unlike those chairs you sit on at restaurants that have one leg shorter than the other—so you stuff a few napkins under it so it stops wobbling—Jesus won't shake or break under any weight you put on Him. And if He won't break or shake, you have no reason to fear that He will let you down. You won't crumble, and neither will He. You can have that assured hope today.

When we taste and see the goodness of God and actually begin to believe that He Himself is faithful, the only reasonable response is to place our faith in Him. Faith is a reasoning trust! But we must also remember that our faith will always require an element of *faith*. Real action. Real steps of trust. Real surrender and submission to the unknowns Jesus is calling us to follow Him into. There will be moments in our walk with Jesus where we go through things that make no sense, that break our hearts, and that turn our world upside down; we will wonder if God is really God-ing up there. The horizon might get a little blurry, and we might not be able to see ten steps ahead like we did in the last season, but that's where faith comes in. We reach out our hand, we trust God to guide us through the dark, and we step where He tells us to step, knowing He would never lead us into the hands of the Evil One (Jeremiah 29:11). He will be our defender and protector, our Savior and friend, and our hope, peace, and joy, leading us to the other side.

He is not like humanity, which is prone to failure, deception, and imperfection. He is victorious, truthful, and perfect. Give Him your hands and allow Him to lead you. Give Him your hope, and He will prove Himself true to you. You don't need crutches when it comes to faith in Christ. He will hold you, heal you, and help you to take those first faith steps today, broken feet and all.

It's Time to Raise Your Banner

As we dare to live lives of hope, we must also dare to live lives of trust. We can trust that life will life, but we can also trust that our Lord will lord. As we call into remembrance His personhood, promises, patterns, and presence, we can rest in faith, hope, joy, and peace, knowing He redeems, repurposes, restores, and renews. As much as this book is a launchpad for you to run the race well, to struggle without strife, and to endure with the expectancy of God's faithfulness to show up, you are also invited to simply rest. Scripture even says that God gives rest to those whom He loves, and, friend—He loves you (Psalm 127:2).

It is no longer all on you to be the strong one. You can let your perfect and present Father, who loves you and holds the whole world in His hands, carry you and everything burdening you today. I think it is also time that you unroll the fabric of your life before Him and allow Him to get to work on fashioning for you a story marked by His glory—to snip, sew, repair, and even slightly tear specific parts and pieces so things fit together as He intended.

Allow Him to stitch together what needs to be mended; to prune and hem what has been dragging at the bottom for too long; to cut and tailor what no longer is fitting your life; to patch over the holes that got caught and snagged on sharp edges; and to add patterns and buttons and rhinestones and sequins where He is ready to reflect color into your life. Let Him *Project Runway* the fabric of your life into a makeshift masterpiece that only He, as the Author, Designer, and Creator of all life, could make! Then bravely and boldly wear it into the world or wave it above you like a banner in a battle well won, because we serve a God of victory and redemption. The world needs to see this. We need to know this.

Now it's time to raise up joy in your life where there was once despair, because we know the God who fashions our fabrics to be heralds of hope.

Now it's time to prop up peace in your life where there was anxiety and fear, because we know the God who protects and surrounds us.

Now it's time to display faith in your life where doubts and lies distract your mind, because we now know the God of truth and faithfulness.

Now it's time to fly your banner of hope in your life where you thought it was over, because we know the God who redeems and brings light to the darkest parts of our lives.

Keep enduring, keep believing, and keep hoping, friend. And if you ever need to fix your eyes on the fabric of hope, or need a reminder of His goodness, you know what book to reopen. It's always here for you; I'm always here for you. But in even better news, God is always there for you, stitching hope into every part of your story.

ACKNOWLEDGMENTS

If you are reading the acknowledgments, man, you are a real one! And the people I will acknowledge in this section are real ones as well!

Thank you to my best friend and husband, Richard. You are the love of my life. I don't think I will ever get over just how good God is that He gave me a man like you to lead me in life and love every part of me unconditionally. Every broken part of me that was shattered by others, you have stepped in and helped heal. You have been such a key piece of the puzzle of God's redemptive work in my own life, and I will never be able to express just how much that means to me. I am a more healed, more whole, and more secure woman who can hope because of the man you are. You are a hero of hope to me, and I love you so much.

To one of my favorite ministry leaders, authors, and mentors, Hosanna Wong—I love you, girl. Your willingness to pull up a seat for me at your table and walk me through the ins and outs of being a

Acknowledgments

woman in ministry and publishing has been such a gift—a gift that will keep on giving, because, as I received your wisdom and advice, I can now pour more effectively into the lives of others who need this message of hope and healing. I want to be you when I grow up. I love you.

I want to honor my friends who shared their stories with me and trusted me to steward them in this book for the hope and healing of you, the reader. I also want to honor those friends who impacted me so that I could impact you through this book.

First, to Hannah Adeoye: We truly are cut from the same fabric, friend. I love you with my entire heart, and I am so proud of the brave and bold woman you are. You do everything with excellence, without compromise, and without complaint. You are truly a Proverbs 31 woman through and through, and I know that God will honor every sacrifice you make to serve and love those around you, family or not. I also honor you for how you have cared for your mother. You have taken on a burden that is not a light load, and I specifically pray that God would not only work a miracle in her life but also grace you with community that would step in and lift your arms as you see little victories in her life every day. You're the best, Hannah. Let's play *Mario Party* soon and sing about Monty Mole.

Second, to Stefanie Rouse: Your willingness to let me share the hard parts of your story is an honor I do not take lightly. You are such an inspiration to me, and I am challenged and moved by the faith and joy you have in God. You and Caleb are some of the most genuine people I know, and I pray that God blesses you both immensely in your marriage, your ministry, and in the lives of

Acknowledgments

future generations that will come after you. Whether it be through your own children or you both rising up to mother and father those who have nobody to love and lead them in their lives, I know God will move mightily in you both to have a lasting legacy and kingdom impact.

Third, to Michael Mims: I needed that Steve Carter book so bad, dude. You saw me in my grief through the phone screen and did more for me than some people who walk next to me in real life. I am forever grateful to you for connecting me to your mentor, and for being the silent, unseen servant who loves all your friends so intentionally. I honor you, Michael, and I pray that, in whatever ways you need hope and healing today, the Lord would bless you and keep you.

Fourth, to my community of friends who have supported me behind the scenes with the writing of this book and the life I lived that was recorded in these pages, I love y'all: Stefany and Eric Luna, Elizabeth Evans, Ashley Rose, Nick and Chelsea Hurst, Jaron and Courtney Haas, Chloee and Tywon Burnom, Ashley Crismon, Jacob and Julia Petersen, Joe Navarro, Chelsea and Preston Kulb, Ali Prado, Craig and Jessica Brown, Robbi Jan, Scott and Keeley Ellis, Faith Womack, Josh and Sydney Benson, Jasmine and Josh Pernell, Tara Snyder, Jacob and Bailey Nwangwa, and Nadia and Elliott Van Dyke.

To my family, I want to say thank you from the bottom of my heart. I wouldn't have been able to carry the burdens of life I have endured without your love and support. Dj, Cj, Kym, Skarlett, Shelly, Grandpa Doyle, Nana Dotty, Uncle Jimmy, Emily Kelly,

Acknowledgments

Rachel Kelly, Grace Kelly, Olga and Pat Kelly—I am so grateful God allowed us to be family. I pray the words in this book prove just how good God has been to us all!

I also want to give a special shout-out to my team who helps me in everything I do: Trinity, Lisa-Jo, Brooke, Meg, Lauren, Allison, and everyone at W. Y'all are *rock stars*! Seriously, can we publish books together forever? You are such a dream team, and I am grateful for how kindly you have walked alongside me in the hardest seasons of my life. Thank you for being some of the best cheerleaders in the biggest achievements of my life. This book wouldn't have been possible without your help, prayers, and encouraging comments on my drafts.

And to my booking agent, John Michael: You are seriously a godsend. The fact that you believe so much in me and in what God has called me to do as an evangelist in this generation makes me feel so seen and loved. I appreciate all your hard work, dedication, and consistent help and hype in everything I do. Let's keep changing lives for the gospel—freedom, hope, and everything in between!

NOTES

CHAPTER 2

1. Coca-Cola, "Coca-Cola Captures Passion for Celebration in New Global Commercials for 2010 FIFA World Cup," press release, April 19, 2010, https://investors.coca-colacompany.com/news-events/press-releases/detail/158/coca-cola-captures-passion-for-celebration-in-new-global-commercials-for-2010-fifa-world-cuptm.
2. K'naan, "Wavin' Flag," track 7 on *Troubadour*, Interscope Records, 2009.
3. John M. Cunningham, "K'Naan," *Britannica*, accessed August 16, 2025, https://www.britannica.com/biography/KNaan.
4. Rick W. Byargeon, "Banner," in *Eerdmans Dictionary of the Bible*, ed. David Noel Freedman et al. (W. B. Eerdmans, 2000), 147.
5. Geoffrey W. Bromiley, ed., "Jehovah-Nissi," in *The International Standard Bible Encyclopedia, Revised* (W. B. Eerdmans, 1979–1988), 980.
6. Douglas K. Stuart, *Exodus*, vol. 2, *The New American Commentary* (Broadman & Holman Publishers, 2006), 401.
7. Kelly Richman-Abdou, "Kintsugi: The Centuries-Old Art of

Notes

Repairing Broken Pottery with Gold," My Modern Met, September 20, 2024, https://mymodernmet.com/kintsugi-kintsukuroi/.

8. Zia Meyer, "Wabi-Sabi: The Japanese Art of Finding the Beauty in Imperfections," Carnegie Library, accessed August 16, 2025, https://www.carnegielibrary.org/staff-picks/wabi-sabi-the-japanese-art-of-finding-the-beauty-in-imperfections/.

CHAPTER 3

1. Helen Briggs, "DNA Story of When Life First Gave Us Lemons," BBC News, February 8, 2018, https://www.bbc.com/news/science-environment-42960445; Jerry James Stone, "History of Lemons—What Am I Even Eating?!," Jerry James Stone, November 13, 2023, https://jerryjamesstone.com/how-to/history-of-lemons-what-am-i-even-eating/.

CHAPTER 4

1. Murray J. Harris, "2 Corinthians," in *The Expositor's Bible Commentary: Romans Through Galatians*, ed. Frank E. Gaebelein, vol. 10 (Zondervan Publishing House, 1976), 397.
2. John Piper, *Desiring God: Meditations of a Christian Hedonist* (Multnomah Books, 1996), 216. Used by permission, www.desiringGod.org.
3. Nancy Leigh DeMoss, *A Place of Quiet Rest: Finding Intimacy with God Through a Daily Devotional Life* (Moody, 2000), 234–35.

CHAPTER 5

1. Gordon Bridger, *The Message of Obadiah, Nahum and Zephaniah: The Kindness and Severity of God*, ed. Alec Motyer and Derek Tidball, The Bible Speaks Today (InterVarsity Press, 2010), 118.
2. Titanic Museum Attraction, "Step Aboard the Titanic Museum Attraction," accessed August 17, 2025, https://titanicattraction.com/.

Notes

3. Pedro C. Ribeiro, "Sinking the Unsinkable: Lessons for Leadership," NASA, August 2, 2012, https://appel.nasa.gov/2012/08/02/sinking-the-unsinkable-lessons-for-leadership/.
4. Aodhán King and Hillsong Young & Free, "Highs and Lows," track 17 on *III*, Sparrow and Hillsong Music, 2018.
5. Forrest Frank with Caleb Gordon, "God Is Good," track 10 on *Child of God*, River House Records, 2024.

CHAPTER 6

1. Artur Weiser, *The Psalms: A Commentary* (The Westminster Press, 1962), 254.

CHAPTER 7

1. Alex Osiadacz, "Mayo Clinic Minute: What Is a Subarachnoid Hemorrhage?," Mayo Clinic, September 16, 2022, https://newsnetwork.mayoclinic.org/discussion/mayo-clinic-minute-what-is-a-subarachnoid-hemorrhage/.
2. Tim Keller, *The Reason for God: Belief in an Age of Skepticism* (Penguin Group, 2008), xvii.
3. Paul Tillich, *Systematic Theology*, vol. 2 (University of Chicago Press, 1957), 116.
4. J. C. Ryle, *Holiness* (James Clarke & Co., 1877).
5. Philip Yancey, *Disappointment with God: Three Questions No One Asks Aloud* (Zondervan, 1988), 117.

CHAPTER 8

1. Term coined by Squire Rushnell in his book *When God Winks*, https://godwinks.com/pages/about-whats-a godwink?.
2. Steve Carter, *Grieve, Breathe, Receive: Finding a Faith Strong Enough to Hold Us* (W Publishing, 2024).
3. Kirby Kelly, host, *Bought and Beloved with Kirby Kelly*, podcast, "Grieve with Hope with Steve Carter," Life Audio, December 25,

2024, https://podcasts.apple.com/nz/podcast/grieve-with-hope-with-steve-carter/id1451228314?i=1000681646920.

CHAPTER 9
1. Hulvey, "Holes," track 7 on *COMA*, Reach Records, 2021.
2. James Swanson, *Dictionary of Biblical Languages with Semantic Domains: Greek (New Testament)* (Logos Research Systems, Inc., 1997).
3. Swanson, *Dictionary of Bible Languages with Semantic Domains*.
4. John D. Barry et al., *Faithlife Study Bible* (Lexham Press, 2012, 2016), Ps. 46:10.

CHAPTER 10
1. Frank E. Gaebelein et al., *The Expositor's Bible Commentary: Genesis, Exodus, Leviticus, Numbers*, vol. 2 (Zondervan Publishing House, 1990).
2. Brad J. Schoenfeld, "The Mechanisms of Muscle Hypertrophy and Their Application to Resistance Training," *Journal of Strength and Conditioning Research* 24, no. 10 (2010): 2857–72, https://doi.org/10.1519/JSC.0b013e3181e840f3.
3. *Strong's Greek Lexicon*, "Holoklēros," G3648, Blue Letter Bible, accessed August 19, 2025, https://www.blueletterbible.org/lexicon/g3648/kjv/tr/0-1/.

CHAPTER 11
1. Leland Ryken et al., *Dictionary of Biblical Imagery* (InterVarsity Press, 2000), 75.

CHAPTER 12
1. John Piper, "God Is Always Doing 10,000 Things in Your Life," Desiring God, January 1, 2013, https://www.desiringgod.org/articles/god-is-always-doing-10000-things-in-your-life.

NOTES

CHAPTER 13

1. The first three *Star Wars* movies by release date are *A New Hope* (1977), *The Empire Strikes Back* (1980), and *Return of the Jedi* (1983). Produced by Lucasfilm and distributed by 20th Century Fox.

ABOUT THE AUTHOR

Kirby Kelly is a speaker, author, podcast host, and content creator based in Dallas, Texas, who has spent over a decade using digital platforms to equip, empower, and engage a global audience with the truth of the gospel. With a BA in Communication and Biblical Studies from Dallas Baptist University and an MA in Theology, Kirby has built a ministry that blends theological depth with cultural relevance. Her online presence spans Instagram, TikTok, YouTube, and her podcast *Bought + Beloved*, where she helps listeners and viewers deepen their love for God and knowledge of the Word. Kirby has authored two books with W Publishing: *You Can Be Free* and *The Fabric of Hope*. From everyday evangelism to her online uploads, Kirby hopes to see this generation live saved, set free, and sent forth in their unique God-given calling.

ALSO AVAILABLE FROM
KIRBY KELLY

AVAILABLE WHEREVER BOOKS ARE SOLD